# Improbable Love

*My Secret Affair in the 1950s*

## John Wertime

*Printemps Presse*        *Paris*   •   *Alexandria, Virginia*

First Edition

*Library of Congress Cataloging-in-Publication Data*

Wertime, John T.
   Improbable Love: My Secret Affair in the 1950s / John T. Wertime. — 1st ed.
      ISBN 978-0-9834388-0-9
      1. Personal memoir. 2. Wertime, John. 3. Fairlington.
      4. Fathers and sons. 5. Mothers and sons. 6. Male
      sexual maturation. 7. Sexual relationships: older women
      and adolescent males. 8. American life: early 1940s
      to late 1960s.

*Library of Congress Control Number:* 2011927010


Note: The names Kimberly, Bruce, Jill, and Martie Blake used in this book are pseudonyms, as is Todd Johnson. Any relationship these fictitious names may have to persons, living or dead, is entirely coincidental.

Designed by John Wertime and Arthur Feller, with a contribution by Nathan Lorentz.

*Published in the United States of America*
*Printemps Presse*
*P. O. Box 16038*
*Alexandria, Virginia 22302-8038*

*http://www.printempspresse.com*

*Printed in the United States of America and other countries.*

for the ones who believed

# Contents

# Improbable Love

The Fourth of July sky was stellar. The moon and stars lit the way, while down below fireflies put on a pyrotechnic show and the cicadas of the forest played a serenade. On this night, Kimberly Blake and her daughters walked down a lane with their friend hosting them at his family's mountain retreat. Despite the calm beauty and sweet summer air, danger lurked in the form of venomous snakes. Beyond the bend in the road, the water of a now soft and sensual pond glimmered, inviting them to swim. Too tired for that, the Blake girls declined, but their mother was game. She helped them get ready for bed in the old log cabin and their friend guided them to the outhouse off to its side. Then she headed with him to the pond.

Stopped in her tracks by the incredible sky, Kimberly stood in awe as he plunged in. He swam around to the back of the float and removed his suit. "Kim! Come on in, the water's fantastic!" he shouted. Hurrying up, she swam to his side and into his arms. Treading water and kissing, he pulled down her suit and grabbed her breasts, which made her laugh excitedly. Bare and free in the fresh water, they whooped and hollered. While in a tight embrace, he probed her crotch, but Kimberly said, very quietly, "My love, I'd like nothing better, but we can't do it here. There's too great a risk." She pulled up her suit and they contented themselves with swimming and reveling.

Hearing the racket, one of the girls awoke and suddenly appeared at the end of the dock. "Jill, come and join us" cried the friend. "The water's terrific!" Kimberly followed with a motherly plea, "Jillilee, get your suit on and come on in. You won't regret it!" Jill's eyes fastened on the two of them as they frolicked in the pitch-black water. She wouldn't budge from her lookout, so after a while, he swam behind the float and put on his trunks.

The next morning, walking toward the upper house to see if breakfast was ready, the Blakes' host encountered his aunt coming down to the water. Besides her swimsuit, she was wearing an enormous smile. "You and Kimberly seem to have had a good time in the pond last night," his aunt said, her eyes sparkling bright like the moon and stars the night before. What she thought her seventeen-year-old nephew and his thirty-five-year-old guest had been up to wasn't clear to him in 1958, or even many years later.

A boy in his mid-teens is very unlikely to become the intimate companion and clandestine lover of a woman nearly the age of his mother, but I did. What prepared me for such a life? How did it happen to come about? Would a relationship like ours be immoral, illegal, exploitative, or damaging? Or could it be true love? As I reveal my story of long ago, and ponder its influence on me, I ask you to come to your conclusions. I've finally arrived at mine.

Johnny, circa 1950.

# Part I — *Innocence*

## 1  Fairlington

My family and I moved into the Arlington, Virginia neighborhood of Fairlington at the end of 1946. Kimberly Blake, her naval officer husband, and two young children arrived there seven years later. Another three years would pass before I met her. In those days, the magnificent trees now lining the way from my old home to the house in which the Blakes came to dwell were still small or not yet planted.

Fairlington was one of several developments in the Washington, D.C., area built by the Federal Government to meet an escalating demand for housing during the early years of World War II. Our planned community of rental units was laid out in two sections, one on either side of a highway running south from Washington toward Richmond. During my first years in Fairlington, Shirley Highway (Route 395) was still a dirt roadbed a little beyond Shirlington, the small shopping center at the bottom of Fairlington's high hills.

South Fairlington, the section in which I lived, was intended primarily for military officers, government employees, and their families; enlisted men and their families found lodging mostly in North Fairlington, with its greater number of apartment buildings. As soon as my father was discharged from his two-year stint in the Army and OSS duty in the Far East, he went to work for the State Department. This made us eligible for inclusion on Fairlington's long waiting list.

When our turn came, Dad was living and working in Washington, while my mother and I and my younger brothers, Dick and Steve, resided in Dad's hometown in Pennsylvania, not far from his mother's house. I remember the excitement I felt at seeing our new home and well-kept neighborhood, which contrasted with the quarters we occupied in "Cardboard Village," a development erected quickly and inexpensively during the war for soldiers and their families.

4

In our early years in Fairlington, there were few cars and little traffic. Most men, including Dad, boarded the bus to go to work at the Pentagon several miles up Shirley Highway, or in Federal buildings not far beyond in the District of Columbia. Its convenient location, spacious grounds, and neo-colonial style red brick buildings with slate roofs made Fairlington a pleasant place. Unfortunately, in those days of segregation, it was open only to whites.

Until Fairlington was sold and converted into individually owned condominiums in the early 1970s, it was a community in a true sense. Hot water for washing and radiator heat came to each building and unit through underground pipes from strategically located power houses. Neighbors shared a coin-operated washer and dryer in the communal half of the basement that ran the length of each building. Mothers pushed infants and toddlers around the sidewalks connecting the houses in the front and back courts, and conversed on their porches or back door stoops while watching their young ones crawl on the lawn or play in the dirt.

My brothers and I occupied the big bedroom that stretched across the upstairs of our stone fronted house. My bed was closest to the

A stone fronted house like ours in Fairlington.

front dormer window. Next came Dick's bed, then Steve's when he outgrew his crib. We played mostly in the first floor bedroom we used as a playroom, or outside on the lawns. Mother lovingly held as many of us on her lap as she could while reading aloud. When we had a hard time falling asleep, she would sit on the side of the bed, stroke our heads, and sing to each of us in her beautiful voice.

What I remember best about our bedroom is the small record player that sat on a dresser by the front window, and some of the music and stories we played. My favorite album was Basil Rathbone's narration of the story of Robin Hood, which I received one Christmas when many of our relatives gathered to celebrate at Grandma Wertime's home. I also listened to classical music that complemented the bouts of melancholy I experienced as I sat looking out my window at dusk, lost in my feelings of the sadness of life and fighting to ward off tears.

Later, when we had a record player that took 45 RPM's, I would play the pop tunes I had bought. One I liked best still rings in my ears—the high pitched voice of a young black boy singing:

*I love you baby and I want you to be my girl.*

A strong desire for someone of my own to hold and to love came to me early in life.

My father had little tolerance for any music not classical. Whenever he heard this music blaring, he'd shout, "Turn that crap off!" Then I'd have to turn it off or way down so he couldn't hear it.

Those of us old enough to be out on our own hit or threw a ball, played hide-and-seek, cowboys and Indians, hopscotch, jump rope, war with toy soldiers, or dolls. No one bothered to lock the doors of houses or cars, or feared for the safety of children outside. The people I encountered were usually kind. I grew up with a strong sense of trust and faith in the goodness of adults, just as they, in turn, generally trusted our government and president to tell them the truth.

As we grew, my brothers, friends, and I played in nearby courts, then in ones all over South Fairlington and some in North Fairlington as well. To get to the other side, we could cross a bridge, the lightly traveled four lane Shirley Highway, or crawl through a large drainage pipe that ran underneath it. In the vine-covered trenches of what remained of one of the many fortifications that ringed the city of Washington during the Civil War, we reenacted recent battles of the South Pacific with our toy guns and gun sounds. In Fairlington, and even alone in downtown Washington, I felt safe and secure.

Close to our house was the elementary school my brothers Dick, Steve, and I attended. Kimberly's daughters would go there, too. Ball fields, tennis courts, and a basketball court weren't far away. Shops and a movie theater lay within walking distance both in Shirlington and in the Fairlington Shopping Centre on the other side of Quaker Lane in Alexandria, between St. Clement's Episcopal Church and Blessed Sacrament Catholic Church. The Co-op, where Mother did her grocery shopping and I often went on my bike in an emergency to buy food for dinner, was located there. Closest of all were friends and neighbors in homes that shared a wall with ours or were a few doors down or across the court. Three girls, who lived opposite us, were our surrogate sisters.

In a woods on the other side of Quaker Lane, my brothers, friends, and I used our Cub Scout hatchets to chop down trees and build lean-tos and tree houses. We gathered up turtles and salamanders to take home for a while, and later on, shot BB guns at targets and sometimes had battles with other children. Wearing nothing more than tiny loin cloths we fashioned from scraps of fabric, a neighbor friend and I once ran through these woods as we imagined Indians had done in earlier times. Soon enough, this nearby remnant of the natural world we loved so much was cleared for new house construction.

Not far from South Fairlington was the Episcopal High School for Boys. Braddock Road, which bordered it on the north, was still quite rural. With Dick and me sitting on a crossbar and Steve in a front basket, our parents took us on bike rides past another overgrown Civil War fortification. The big dogs that lived in the few houses along the road terrified me when they ran after us, nipping at our heels.

Off the dirt roadbed of Shirley Highway were the remnants of old farms, where blackberry bushes abounded, Holmes Run flowed, and one could encounter an unpenned sow menacingly protective of her litter. Here and anywhere else nature still existed within walking distance of our home, Dad led us on hikes. With Steve on his shoulders, he set a brisk pace Mother, Dick, and I had to hustle to maintain. The completion of Shirley Highway brought rapid development and change to the landscape of the whole area, eventually forcing us to go farther afield for our walks in the country.

From time to time gypsies came to Fairlington. Working in tandem, one would knock on the front door during the day to distract the lady of the house while another woman slipped in the unlocked back door in search of something of value. On occasion, as I experienced, several men pulled up in a big car and asked a pedestrian to change a large bill one of them dangled out the window, hoping to snatch an unsuspecting person's cash and drive away.

The sound of two very different kinds of bells brought Fairlington residents out in an flash. One belonged to the Good Humor Man, who would drive into every parking lot on summer evenings to be mobbed by children and their parents.

The other came from the poor soul we children dubbed Da Da, Da Munji, once an Italian prisoner-of-war incarcerated in this country. Every so often, he appeared carrying his foot-powered grinding wheel, ringing his bell, and shouting something that sounded to us kids like the name we gave him. Walking from court to court, he stopped whenever someone needed him to sharpen a knife or pair of scissors. We loved to watch him at work and hear him try to communicate with customers in an accent we could barely comprehend. Once he started on his way, we followed him as if he were the Pied Piper, all the while crying out, "Da da, da munji, da da, da munji!" Turning back, he'd raise his fist and shout at us, "*Somma botch! Somma botch!*"

The abundance of children we encountered on moving into Fairlington shortly before Christmas 1946 was a preview of what was to come. We were all young then, my parents twenty-seven, I five-and-a-half, Dick a year-and-a-bit younger, and Steve not quite four years my junior. Charles wouldn't be born until 1952. Getting married young and quickly starting a family was not uncommon in those days. Birth control consisted primarily of the diaphragm, the condom, or abstinence. Abortion was illegal, expensive and often dangerous. If someone forgot or the contraceptives failed, the consequences were lasting, whether desired or not. Young parents like mine grew up with their children, hoping to reach maturity first.

## 2  Dad

My father, Theodore ("Ted") Wertime, was working as a China analyst in the State Department's Research and Intelligence division when we came to our new Fairlington home. His mind was lightning fast, his appetite for learning voracious, and his ability to absorb and synthesize amazing. Handsome, with brown hair and blue eyes, a strong jaw, straight nose, and a good physique, my 5'10" father was capable of great charm for the right people. Unfortunately, when he returned home from work, he underwent a radical personality transformation into lord of the family manor with a short fuse and bad temper.

Dad met Mother during a German poetry reading in the home of his German professor at Haverford College, where he was a student and my mother had come for the occasion from nearby Bryn Mawr College. With her striking blond hair, good looks, and 5'7" height, Bernice "Peggy" Schultz immediately attracted the attention of this brash young man, who soon won her heart. I was born in Washington, D.C., on April 9, 1941, nine months after their wedding in Trenton, New Jersey. At the time, my father was finishing up his M.A. in history at American University.

Dad's energy seemed limitless. During his lunch break at work, he went to the Library of Congress to continue historical research which a growing family had caused him to abandon while a Ph.D. candidate at Johns Hopkins. At home, he pursued his scholarship at night and on the weekend, along with his passion for the violin and viola, which he often practiced at odd hours. He enjoyed refinishing antique furniture, biking, hiking, and playing sports with us. In between all this and occasional housework to help Mother, he kept up a voluminous correspondence with various scholars and friends. Frequent short naps during the day and at night refreshed him and kept him going.

When Dick and I in our younger years disturbed our father's

sleep, reading, writing, or music practice, he often flew into a rage. "Quiet! I told you to be quiet!" he'd shout, then he'd bound up the stairs to where we were playing or scuffling and pummel us. Unless we held on to the bannister tightly enough, he'd shove or boot us down the uncarpeted stairs. During these spontaneous assaults, our nearly hysterical mother would scream, "Stop it, Ted, Stop it!" but dared not intervene. What Grandma Wertime told our mother early in her marriage, "Peggy, I've learned never to cross a man," was advice she didn't forget.

Our mother encouraged and supported us in whatever we did, and helped where she could, while often forgoing her own pleasures. She had three, then four, sons to care for, and in our highly impatient, demanding, and self-centered father, the equivalent workload of a couple more.

Mother had to assure that Dad's clothes were ready in the morning so he could get off to work on time, and that dinner was prepared when he returned. On many a morning, especially when I was younger, I woke up to various barked questions and demands, such as, "Peg! Where're my shorts?", "Tie my tie!", or "Why haven't

Fairlington in 2011 (now on the National Register of Historic Places and a Virginia Landmark Historic District) looks almost as it did when we arrived in 1946.

you ironed my shirt?"

Besides doing the laundry, ironing, shopping, and cleaning, which I helped with in various ways, Mother was our father's typist, a job she began while she was still at Bryn Mawr, continued during Dad's graduate school days, and performed until the end of his life. "Peg, how much typing did you do today?" was one of the first questions he asked when he got home from work in the evening. Dad never took the time to learn to type. Our mother was the rare person who could decipher his nearly illegible handwriting. When she fell behind, he'd chew her out and say, "I don't care if you have to stay up till midnight. I want the typing done by the time I'm home from work tomorrow!"

Mother had problems budgeting the hours of the day and being on time, a tendency compounded by the demands we all made on her and the difficulty she had in refusing any of them. "Come on, Peg, we're going to be late!" was one of several refrains we heard throughout the house over the years.

Our mother was a competent pianist, with whom our father liked to play sonatas. From time to time, he also wanted her to accompany his string quartet when it performed in our small living room. Besides household chores, typing, and frequent marital duties, which required Mother to drop everything when Dad came in from work and disappear into their bedroom for a few minutes while we clamored about, he expected her to be in top form on the piano. "Did you practice today?" was a question he also asked upon entering the house. Though he did little to help make this possible, our musical scholar father, the son of a music professor who studied in the native Germany of his own, Jewish immigrant, father, didn't countenance errors gracefully. "No, no!" he'd growl. "You made a mistake! Let's go back to the last bar and start over."

In her irrepressible way, Mother sometimes sat down and played a jazzy popular tune. This irritated Dad. He'd scowl, and exclaim, "For Christ's sake, Peg, cut that out!", or simply say, "Oh, shit!", and walk away in disgust. With her sunny disposition and enthusiasm for life, Mother could also burst out in song or do the can-can in front of us, which Dad didn't much appreciate either. Such reprimands, coupled with his expectation of complete silence in the house when he practiced, did little to endear the musical scene to me.

12

In his professional work and historical research, our father was eminently rational. What he did at the State Department and later at the United States Information Agency (USIA) earned the respect of his colleagues. In time, his independent scholarly efforts brought him international recognition in the field of early metallurgy and pyrotechnology—humankind's use of fire to mold materials. However, when it came to chores at home and the exercise of his authority, the sheen of reasonableness disappeared. Much of his communication with us was indirect and came in the form of an order to our mother to tell the boys to do this or that.

Sometimes the order came directly from him, as it did one winter night when he came home from work and asked if we'd washed our station wagon that afternoon. Because it was bitter cold, all three of us answered we hadn't yet done the job, but would once it warmed up a bit. Our unacceptable response brought on his typical angry facial gesture of teeth tightly clenched and a strong jaw thrust forward, followed by a barked command, "I told you to do that! Get out and do it now!" Still too young to disobey, Dick, Steve, and I washed the car as best we could in the dark. As the warm water we carried out in buckets hit the cold metal and glass, it turned to ice, encasing our station wagon in a solid sheet that glistened in the moonlight.

Not all chores were assigned, for each of us brothers had a paper route starting at the age of eight or nine. Mine was the first. The *Arlington Daily*, a new local paper, advertised on the radio for carriers ready to start new routes. Although I was dressed in my Cub Scout uniform for the Pack meeting at seven that night, I decided to skip it and try my hand at soliciting for customers. My new route started off with the seven subscribers I signed up in the couple of hours I spent knocking on doors. As I got older, I was able to get bigger routes, including ones delivering the *Times Herald* in the morning, then the *Evening Star* in the afternoon. On a number of cold, blustery, and snowy Sunday mornings, Mother or Dad helped out by following us in the station wagon with newspapers piled high in the back. Pulling a wagon filled with papers she stacked around our little brother, Mother also delivered for us in emergencies during the week. Paperboys in those days were responsible for collecting subscription fees and dealing with the complaints of angry customers. While not always pleasant, such encounters gave us a good introduction to the world of business and finance.

When I could, I also did odd jobs for the neighbors, such as vacuuming, scrubbing and waxing flours, washing windows, and babysitting. Two of the children I sat for, toddler girls, were immediate neighbors. I had a lot of experience caring for my brother, Charlie, and changing his diapers quickly so I didn't get squirted in the face. Changing girls' diapers, at first an unaccustomed chore for a boy with no sisters, turned out to be a less risky affair.

During the first number of years we lived in Fairlington, the paltry salary the State Department paid my father was barely adequate to support our family. To save money, Dad was the family barber. He'd sit on the toilet seat in the bathroom and hold us on his lap with the admonition, "Hold still!" while he used his hand clippers on us. If we moved the slightest or his hand wasn't perfectly steady, the clippers would pull our hair, a sensation that was quite painful, bordering on traumatic. When the ordeal was over, he'd tell us to get the dustpan and brush and sweep up. For years, he sheared us this way. As we became more self-conscious of our appearance, we balked at his hairstyling, and finally asked for money, or used our paper route earnings, for a professional haircut, something we felt proud to have. Going to the barbershop became a rite of passage out of childhood for my brothers and me.

With his many activities and interests, Dad tended to be too busy to bother with money matters, responsibility for which he left to Mother. Through my odd jobs and paper route, I built up a small nest egg, from which I made the initial payment on braces for my teeth. I also acted as a private banker to my mother, who handled the family finances. When she was in a pinch, Mother came to me for a loan. "Johnny," she'd say, "I need to borrow twelve dollars [or such]. I'll pay you back as soon as I can." Loving my mother as I did, I was always happy to help her out this way or in any other way I could.

From time to time, Dad would wonder about the family's finances. When he did, he'd query Mother about them. As one of us approached them during these inquests, our parents immediately switched into German, a language Mother majored in and Dad learned well enough to get by. *Geld*, money, and *sagen nichts*, say nothing, were words we dreaded to hear. On their heels came Dad's angry looks and unsuccessful attempts to control his ire, and Mother's proffered explanations and copious tears. Our father's innate frugality and caution with money always clashed with our mother's natural generosity and willingness to take risks.

These blowups as well as Dad's quickness to anger and Mother's penchant for trying to protect us and herself from unpleasant situations helped inculcate secrecy and lying in us. "Don't tell your father about so and so" was an admonition I heard from an early age and took to heart. Later, when my lover used similar words enjoining secrecy, I saw nothing unusual about the request. All that differed was the person in question.

The relentless intensity of life at home was relieved when Dad went away for several months at a time on a State Department mission to the Far East during the Korean War, and later to Vietnam. To celebrate his departure, Mother took us to the Hot Shoppe in Shirlington, where the hamburger platter I ordered always tasted good. During our father's absence, we experienced none of the intellectual fervor he continually exuded. We did, however, get a small taste of how calm and pleasant everyday life must have been for many of our peers. Dad's return brought tales of exotic places and adventure as well as gifts from Hong Kong or Occupied Japan. Typically though, our happiness to see him soon wore thin with the recurrence of the loud demands and commands that punctuated our daily routines.

Dad's radical mood swings had their high points as well as their low. Counterbalancing his violent behavior and unreasonable demands were the many pleasant things he did with us and our friends. He was a great reader and storyteller, who made up "Jonas stories" based on happy days he spent with "Grandpap" on his farm in West Virginia. He took us to football games at the Episcopal High School, and afterwards, to play in its old gymnasium. Going home, we walked on top of the high brick wall that surrounded the school. In early autumn, Dad looked for persimmons that had fallen from a tree that grew along it. When not completely ripe, they turned our mouths inside-out. Even better, he led us on hikes down the unfinished roadbed of Shirley Highway and along the C&O canal on the Maryland side of the Potomac River. "Mr. Wertime, look at this!" or "Mr. Wertime, what's that called?" were frequent sounds on the excursions the neighborhood's most popular father conducted. Unfortunately, what Dad so wonderfully gave with one hand, he often took back with the other.

I loved my father for the many good things he did with me, my brothers, and our friends, but hated his behavior when the bad came to the fore. As a child, I thought the fact that Dad's own father had died when he was only nine helped explain his negative traits. I also saw a certain sense of insecurity and vulnerability under the tough façade he projected, and felt a sense of responsibility for him as well as for my mother and brothers.

Sports were a family preoccupation Dad's highly competitive streak encouraged. Whether to satisfy his needs or ours, he was ready at the drop of a hat for a game of touch football or softball after work or on the weekend. As soon as he could, he gathered us together for a contest and told us to round up our friends. We four, and sometimes Mother, played on the large lawn along Quaker Lane, even in the snow. From an early age, Steve was included, though usually to hike the football or chase stray balls. As he grew, his frustration at his limited role increased. "Why do I always have to hike?" he'd ask in a plaintive voice. Neighborhood kids, girls as well as boys, and occasionally their parents, joined us. When we played football, our father removed his shoes to drop kick, which impressed our friends. The long ball Dad hit through a neighbor's dining room window just before dinner one evening did, however, put a damper on our soft ball games.

For my brothers and me, baseball was a consuming passion and our main diversion during the summer. Long before we were old enough to play on a team, we wore baseball hats and uniforms throughout the day and often to bed. Early in our lives, we started to follow the major leagues in the papers, on the radio, and as collectors of trading cards, of which we had stacks and stacks. I was a Boston Red Sox fan who idolized

16

Ted Williams, whose autograph I once got at Fenway Park in Boston on a trip with two of Dad's colleagues. To my irritation, Dick rooted for the Red Sox's nemesis, Joe DiMaggio, and the New York Yankees, but Steve sided with me. Only a thunderstorm or heavy snowfall kept us from throwing a ball or hitting some type of sphere in the court behind our house, or along Quaker Lane.

As time went by, organized sports started to take over from our neighborhood pick up games, but didn't fully supplant them. The first team experience we had was in the Cub Scout softball league. Dad pitched to us in batting practice before our Saturday morning contests, watched us play, and in time coached a team. Then came Little League and Junior League baseball, and the flag football league our former Cub Scout master, Budge Harding, organized and refereed. During the basketball season when I was twelve, my team played in an old gym, which my father realized once belonged to a finishing school for young women the Army took over during the Second World War. Kimberly herself, I later learned, played in that gym as a student. Throughout all of this, our mother was a faithful fan, and chauffer, too, once she got her driver's license.

Next to school, sports constituted the dominant factor in our lives. In fact, sports became so important that Dad made a career decision with them in mind. At the Department of State, he faced increasing pressure to take a foreign assignment, a move he knew would significantly impact our ability to pursue the sports we loved. Mother and Dad conferred and agreed it would be better for us to remain at home through high school. When an opportune time came, he moved over to the United States Information Agency in Washington.

## 3 Mom's Latest Career

"Mom's latest career" was a standing joke between my brothers and me. Our mother had so many careers it was hard for us to keep track of them. This was not due to any lack of talent or determination on her part, but because the family depended on her for so many things that she couldn't be away for long before her absence impinged on our comforts and needs.

Mother's modeling career was her first. When Dad and Larry Gruits, an Army Major, went abroad about the same time in 1950, Mother invited Kitty, Larry's wife, to join her in taking a three-month self-improvement and modeling course advertised in the *Washington Post*. Every Tuesday, she and Kitty boarded the bus for downtown Washington and their class, and every week they got a paying work assignment somewhere in the area.

In the afternoon on the days when my mother was away pursuing her new career, I'd wait at home for her to return, first, patiently, then longingly, all the while becoming more and more anxious. When it got really late, I'd sit on some steps across the street from the bus stop, crying quietly to myself for fear the mainstay of my life wouldn't appear. With each bus that pulled up to the stop, my hopes rose, only to be dashed when she didn't step out, causing me to sink into deeper despair. At last I'd see my mother's sparkling blond hair and smiling face as she crossed the street once the bus had moved on down the road. Nothing could match the sense of relief and happiness that overcame me watching her come toward me with outstretched arms.

Drying my tears, I'd say, "Mom, I thought you'd never come home!"

"Sweetheart, you know I'd never go off and leave you and your brothers," my mother always assured me.

18

One of her class assignments was to demonstrate artificial fingernails at Woodward & Lothrop, a leading Washington department store. In turn, this brought her an offer to do the same on TV. To watch this impressive event, my brothers and I went to a neighbor's home. The commercial was short and our mother was good. But with no more opportunities, her modeling career ended there.

The first time Mother tried her hand at sales was when I was ten. For a few months, she sold the six-volume *Child's World* in Fairlington door to door. When she had earned $260 and a free set of these books, she made a down payment on our first car.

During the same year, she got a job selling dresses at Jelleff's, a ladies' clothing store in Shirlington. Her work hours caused problems with feeding us boys, so a couple of times, Jen Jones, the wife of one of our father's State Department colleagues who had grown up in China with his missionary parents, offered to have us to dinner. On one occasion, while we sat around in the living room waiting to eat, Jen ordered her husband to put down his newspaper and vacuum the house. With an Oriental sort of calm, he kept on reading despite his wife's repeated demands. The exact opposite of our own parents, our hostess flew into a rage as her husband sat there motionless, grinning like a Cheshire cat at his young and highly discomfited guests. We'd never seen a man and woman interact that way before. After about six weeks, Mother was laid off because the manager had hired too many sales clerks. All of us were relieved to have her home.

For several years, my youngest brother's birth prevented our mother from pursuing work that required a daily commitment. When I was in the sixth grade and Dick in the fifth, we used our paper route money to buy the *World Book Encyclopedia* in installments. After that, our mother decided to sell these books herself. Over a period of nine months, she made $390, which she put toward braces for teeth.

By Charlie's fourth birthday, Mother was ready for another career. The first job she found was teaching a nursery school class Charlie could attend at the Fairlington Presbyterian Church. Our car was in the parking lot, but she didn't have a driver's license, so she and Charlie had to walk. This lasted for three months, then Mother stepped down. The main benefit to her was the realization that it was time to learn how to drive.

In the spring of 1955, Mother got her learner's permit at the age of thirty-six. The timing was fortunate, because several months after that, I had to get a cast removed from a shoulder injured during a baseball game. Mother offered to drive me to the Anderson Clinic despite her lack of a license. I was desperate to be rid of the hot, smelly cast in the middle of summer, and accepted. We made it to the clinic well enough. On the way home, however, we hit rush hour traffic as we came up a small incline and had to stop at a red light. Mother hadn't fully mastered the car's manual transmission, so we kept sliding backwards toward the cars behind when the light turned green. "Help me, Johnny, help me!" she cried as I crouched down on the floor, mortified and fearful one of my peers would see me in this embarrassing situation. After much honking from the cars behind and several more red lights, Mother finally coordinated both feet and we got up the small hill. Now more determined than ever, she soon got her driver's license, and was ready for another career.

Mindful of the talent she possessed in dealing with people and the rapid pace at which our area was developing, Mother thought real estate would be a good career for her. She contacted a broker who had established her own company in Northern Virginia and was invited to come to work. On the first day in the office, Mother heard that to be successful, she would need a car of her own and a full-time housekeeper. Since we were lucky to have just one car and help in the house once a week, she realized she couldn't continue. Over in a day, this was the shortest of all her careers.

Next came a stint at Woodward & Lothrup, located in a new shopping center at Seven Corners in Fairfax County. Two months later, her boss fired her for being late.

Mother was as inveterate a romantic as she was an optimist. One job that deeply interested her and required no punctuality or help in the house was matchmaking. Her first major success in this field was the lifelong union she arranged between her best friend and classmate at Bryn Mawr and my father's best friend at Haverford, who were married in 1941. Fifteen years later, less consciously, she exercised her matchmaking talents on Kimberly and me.

Another of Mother's callings was encouraging her sons to think big and believe in their dreams. In this, she was inspired by Norman Vincent Peale's *The Power of Positive Thinking*. Mother never tired of telling us what she had read there: "Think big, pray big, and act big."

Late in the summer of 1956, just before I started tenth grade, I saw an ad in the *Washington Post* announcing a scholarship a newspaper carrier could win to the prestigious New England prep school, Phillips Exeter. I showed it to my mother, who repeated Peale's advice once again, and encouraged me to apply. Early in my sophomore year, I was one of the finalists in this contest, or at least one of those an official of the school interviewed. The idea of leaving my large high school for an elite prep school appealed to me, and my mother supported me with assurances that I was special and sure to succeed.

How special I was or wasn't must have become clear to the interviewer rather quickly, particularly after he perused the short essay he asked me to write on the spot. The topic—what I wanted to do or be in the future—wasn't something I'd thought much about. Since I enjoyed making crude designs of buildings and was taking mechanical drawing in school, I wrote that I hoped to become an architect. Spelling was never a strong point of mine, so as we left together, I asked, "Mom, how do you spell architect?" When I heard her answer, I knew my error wasn't a good omen, but my mother assured me the interviewer wouldn't hold this against me. In fact, she so convinced me of my pending success that I started to tell some of my basketball teammates and coaches I wouldn't be returning the following year.

This dream didn't last long. One day toward the end of fall, to her chagrin and my desolation, the mailman delivered a thin envelope containing a single sheet thanking me for my interest and effort. Mother and I had forgotten the advice her mother offered on many occasions, "Remember, don't count your chickens before they hatch."

At the end of August 1956, my mother landed a paying job that suited her temperament and the needs of the family. This was the position of church secretary at St. Clement's, a three-minute walk from our front door. The woman who held it was moving away and recommended Mother to replace her. Following a short interview, the minister hired her on the spot.

Everything was ideal. Her new boss, the Rev. Maurice Henry Hopson, was genial and easygoing, the parishioners were friendly, and Charlie attended preschool upstairs while Mother worked down below in the office next to Mr. Hopson's. She and Charlie arrived at nine and finished at one. When school was over, my brother came downstairs and joined our mother in the kitchen for the lunch she brought along. Then they walked home together and greeted my brothers and me when we returned from school.

Mr. Hopson had been at St. Clement's for seven years when Mother arrived. A dapper bachelor with slightly effeminate mannerisms, he wore a white clerical collar to work and favored tweed jackets. As befitting a cleric, the top of his head had a natural tonsure. His 5'7" height and compact build contrasted strikingly with my own 6'2" lanky frame; so did his thin round tortoiseshell glasses with the thicker black ones I wore to see the blackboard, and hit or shoot a ball. Mr. Hopson and Mother got along famously. She was eager for us to meet the minister, and for him to see the sons she was so proud of.

On the way to his office in the morning, Mr. Hopson would stop by to see Mother and report on the latest events in his life. These usually pertained to the exasperating exploits of his male housemate, who often borrowed his money and car, sometimes with disastrous results. Whenever Charlie came in from the playground with sand in his clothes or shoes, Mr. Hopson grabbed a broom and swept up after him without complaint. His sensitivity, kindness, and compassion endeared him to Mother and the members of his congregation, especially the women.

After working in this job for a few weeks, Mother began to talk to me about a parishioner named Kimberly Blake, who frequently came by the church office. "I want you to meet Kimberly," she told me with the special wide-eyed, anticipatory look she got when matchmaking was in the air. Or I'd hear her say enthusiastically, "You'll love Kim. I can't wait for you to meet her. She's so charming and beautiful!"

The object of Kimberly's weekday visits to the church was the parson himself, whom she affectionately called "Hoppy." From the front office, Mother could overhear Kimberly and Mr. Hopson talking and laughing a lot. Then Kimberly would come out, say goodbye to Mother, and be off in her station wagon.

Soon, Kimberly's visits to St. Clement's included longer and longer stops in the secretary's office, where she and Mother conversed about their families and lives. My mother learned how Kimberly's handsome young naval officer husband, Bruce, had died from cancer of the eye two years earlier. Kimberly was devoted to her two young daughters, who went to Fairlington Elementary School. She was planning to take classes to complete her unfinished B.A., and needed a reliable babysitter during the week, and on the weekend, when she went out with Mr. Hopson. A lonely widow, Kimberly had fallen in love with her pastor, and desperately sought a husband.

Sometimes, Mother dropped by her friend's house to chat. She'd tell Kim how very proud she was of her sons, especially me. I was so mature, responsible, and helpful to her. Whenever she needed something, I was there ready and willing, and would be a good babysitter for her girls. Mother talked of Dick and Steve, of what they both did, and of Charlie, whom Kim already knew, and how I was as much a father to him as a big brother. Her handsome husband, Ted, she'd probably say, was brilliant and passionate, but was always in a hurry. She had little time for herself, but was happy to be the wife of such a fascinating and exciting man and the mother of four wonderful boys.

On a couple of occasions in mid-September, I heard from Mother that I'd just missed seeing Kimberly, who dropped by to say hello. Then, late in the afternoon, one warm, sunny day, my mother and I happened to be outside in front of our house with Charlie when Kimberly pulled up in her car. She wanted to meet me. Looking directly into my face with her sparkling eyes and bright, happy smile, she offered an outstretched hand and said, "Johnny, I'm so happy to meet you at last. Peggy's told me so much about you. You don't know how proud of you she is."

All I had heard about Kimberly still didn't prepare me for the tall, willowly woman who stood before me shaking my hand. I gazed at her full lips, strong chin, and high cheekbones. With bangs in front, her long brown hair was pulled back and wrapped in a bun. She radiated a kind of warmth, exuberance, and sophistication I hadn't experienced before. The look in her eyes and sound of her voice stuck in my mind.

In a word, Kimberly dazzled me.

"Thank you," I replied, after regaining my equilibrium. "I'm glad to meet you, too. Mom talks about you all the time."

Kimberly then leaned forward, touched my arm, and spoke in a earnest tone of voice. "Johnny" she said, "I need someone to sit for my girls, Jill and Martie, a time or two during the week, and sometimes on the weekend. Would you be willing to help me out?"

"Certainly," I said.

"Can you come this Saturday evening from seven to ten? But you probably have a date, don't you?" she asked.

"No. I'm free. I'll be there," I answered.

With newspapers to deliver, I excused myself, and proceeded to the entrance of our parking court, where several bundles of the *Evening Star* sat on the curb waiting for me. By the time I pulled out my wire cutters, clipped open the bundle, and loaded my bag, Kimberly had said goodbye to my mother and brother and was leaving to pick up her girls. She smiled and waved at me, turned left into Stafford Street, and was off.

Our first meeting was brief, but it made a lasting impression on me. Mother was right—I would indeed love Kimberly.

## 4  Women & Girls

Before I met Kimberly, my mother was the woman I knew best. Others, too—my grandmothers, aunts, neighbors, playmates' mothers, and teachers— showed me how and what women think, feel, look like, can be, and do. The girls I knew were from my neighborhood and school, and our visits to relatives' homes, especially Grandma Wertime's, and our Wertime family outings and mountain retreat. I have positive memories of almost all of the women and girls I knew, but none of them influenced me to the extent Kimberly did.

My mother tried to do her best for me, and I was grateful for it, even when there were times it caused me pain. She was very popular in high school. Through diligence and hard work, she had an excellent academic record, better than her older brother, who acknowledged this with the remark, "Huh, smart in school and dumb at home!"

I inherited more of my mother's genes than my father's, which made me tall and slender like her maternal grandfather, Philip Heim, and very blond and fair skinned like my German ancestors who came from East Prussia, along the southeastern Baltic coast. I was so blond that people called me "whitey," "towhead," or "blondie," names that only accentuated my self-consciousness, as did my bright red sun burns common in summer, the color I turned when embarrassed. For years, I longed to have dark hair and a darker complexion, which I found so attractive in others, especially women.

Because of our proximity to Washington, I met people from all over the country. Transplanted Southerners were unmistakable with their distinct accents, intonations, soft, lilting twangs or slight lisps, which I found appealing and at one point imitated in my own speech. Memories of the Civil War enveloped us. Newspapers and magazines published pictures of surviving Union and Confederate veterans and former slaves as well as stories concerning the war and the process of reconciliation still taking place.

No one represented the antebellum South to me better than Mamaw, the maternal grandmother of our neighbors and playmates, "Brother" and "Happy" Lee. A somewhat feisty lady, Mamaw spoke the language of Tennessee. I first met her in their home, and then visited her a few times in her own apartment down the street. Mother and I often joked that it was "The old ladies and babies who liked me best."

The flavor of the Old South, of which Virginia was such a significant part, also came to me in a woman we knew as "Colored Ruth," who helped our mother with the housework once a week for two years. Short and squat with a smiling, moon-shaped face as dark as ours was light, and gold teeth that glistened, Ruth was the granddaughter of slaves. She spoke a brand of English that reminded me of what I heard in stories of Tom Sawyer and Huckleberry Finn that Dad read to us and our neighborhood friends as we lay sprawled on the floor around him. This warm and caring lady used to tell us she was our "black mammy." She loved us and we loved her. While our youngest brother was still small, she bathed him in a small basin in the kitchen sink.

One day Ruth cut her finger while working. As soon as he learned what had happened, three-year old Charlie ran to her. He wanted to see the color of her blood. As she showed him her cut, she said, "See, the Lawd created some of uz black, and some of uz white, but we'se both the same color inside." This impressed Charlie, but he looked concerned. Then he blurted out, "I sure hope I don't turn black!" Ruth roared with laughter. With us, Ruth was free of the horrific bigotry that kept segregation and discrimination alive. The only one in our house whose existence smacked of bondage was unfortunately our mother.

Given the number of children in Fairlington, birthday parties came with great frequency. A party I'll never forget took place when I was eight or nine. Dick and I were invited to the home of a playmate; out of courtesy, so was much younger Steve. One of the games we played involved choosing a mystery object that everyone would try to identify. After all of us had had a turn, our friend's mother called on Steve for his suggestion. Steve thought hard for a minute, and said "dink," which caught Dick and me totally off guard. As we stood there mortified, our hostess, with a quizzical look laced with apprehension, asked, "What's that, Stevie?" Before he could explain, Dick and I jumped in to say it was just some childish talk and changed the subject as quickly as possible. No one knew, of course, that "dink" was the word we'd coined for a female's pudendum when we were still young enough to join our mother in the bathtub.

Besides direct observation of my mother and young female cousins I saw while we stayed at Grandma Wertime's during the war, my early awareness of sexual differences was furthered by firsthand experience. It was when we lived in "Cardboard Village" that I had my first direct contact with a "dink." That was supplied by Christine, a neighbor and playmate five like me, or a year older, under the high outdoor wooden stairs leading up to our living room door. Christine had learned something of the mysteries of life, and was eager to share that knowledge with Dick and me. She pulled up her dress, pulled down her panties, and instructed us to bare ourselves and rub up against her the way big people do when they play "fucky fucky." I don't recollect how many times I underwent this tuition. I do remember enjoying it a lot, despite my apprehension that Mother would catch us in the act.

Much sleeping around and carrying on took place in the "Barracks," as Papa, our maternal grandfather, used to call our community. Men from Fort Ritchie on the Maryland-Pennsylvania line often came to visit women whose husbands were soldiers off fighting the war. Who knows what Christine had seen or done before she took my brother and me under her wing. It would be more than ten years before I had this kind of experience again.

One unusual party I attended was to celebrate the thirteenth birthday of Louis Klechek, an only child a year older than me who lived one court over. A stocky boy with blondish hair, Lewis wore glasses, had asthma, and differed from the rest of us in collecting weapons and pornography, interests he shared with his father. That afternoon, his mom served us ice cream and cake at the dining room table, saw Louis open his presents, then disappeared upstairs while Louis ushered us to the basement to watch a movie. As his father readied the projector, and we kids fidgeted and made wisecracks in anticipation of a cartoon,

Louis stood there watching us with a strange, expectant look on his face. Suddenly, we saw a black and white film flicker, and then come into focus. The first of our birthday shows featured naked women copulating with big dogs with enormous erections, a spectacle we watched in stunned or uncomprehending silence. Being one of the older boys, I understood, and subsequently avoided Louis. Soon thereafter, he and his parents moved away.

Until my family owned a car, we took the local bus into Washington and the Greyhound to visit Grandma Wertime. Less frequently, we boarded the train to see Grandma Schultz, Papa, and our great-grandmother, Jenetta Heim. These visits ended when the three of them left for California in 1947.

For years, Grandma and Papa looked after Grandma's bachelor uncle, Julius Heim, her "Uncle Jule," who made his money in the printing business. When she thought the time was right, my grandmother approached her uncle for help. In appreciation for what they had done for him, he enabled my grandparents to move from a modest house to one an architect designed for them and a New York decorator furnished. He also paid my mother's way to Bryn Mawr College, provided the family with a new car, money for clothes shopping in New York, college and dental school for her brother, stock in Grandma's name, plus a lengthy trip to Europe for mother and daughter. Years later, a generous Grandma Schultz would similarly help my family, although with much more limited means.

My grandmother was a woman with fine and attractive features. She loved to sew, play the piano, sing and dance with her husband, son, and daughter, garden, draw, and paint. Unlike Papa, she never went to college. This bothered Grandma, who didn't like to feel inferior to anyone, including the Queen of England, and expressed this sentiment often, proclaiming, "I'm as good as she is!"

Every few years after their move, Grandma Schultz would come to stay with us in Fairlington for a couple of weeks, bringing clothes she'd sewn for our mother, and helping her with the cooking and housework. Despite abundant energy, Grandma found our activities and Dad's shouting and violin practice during the day and night overwhelming. In exasperation she often exclaimed, "There's never a dull moment around here!" When irritated by the sound of the violin, she would say in a high pitched voice "peep peep peep," roll her eyes, and gesticulate with her hands.

Sex and pleasure never coincided for Grandma Schultz. Her abiding fear of having more than the two children she did wasn't unfounded—the family doctor aborted four additional pregnancies at home. Without this intervention, she would have had as many children as Grandma Wertime, and a very different lifestyle from the one she enjoyed. On many occasions, Grandma expressed her inner feelings by telling me or Dick, "A man has all the fun!" She also let us know that when she wasn't in the mood, she would tell our grandfather, "Not now, Fred," and he'd reply, "Then I'll go have a good pee." Papa had his own trepidations, for he grew up as the oldest child of a large family, and was the principal helper, then supporter, of his widowed mother. As a result, he was given to saying, "More people, more problems," an aphorism Grandma often repeated.

As I learned in various ways over many years, Grandma Schultz's jaundiced view of sex and outspokenness about it may well have had a deleterious influence on her daughter. This did not, however, squelch Mother's romantic dreams or desire for sexual pleasure, even though she never achieved either in her marriage with our impatient and self-centered father, whom she loved deeply despite his many flaws. Dad in turn loved Mother greatly and counted on her help and support as much as her sons did, but never gave her the attention and encouragement she needed and deserved.

During our visits to Trenton in winter, our grandmother, in an unusual twist on bundling, would bring first Dick, then me, into her bed to warm our cold hands by wedging them high up between her bare thighs.

Grandma had a sharp tongue that caused her trouble at times. Once, she almost got fired from a job because of a caustic remark she made to her boss. Her vocabulary included numerous German words and expressions learned as a child who spoke only German with her Lutheran parents in Brooklyn until the age of five. She amused or mortified us with these and an array of English and German aphorisms, curses, and epithets, both racial and religious. If she thought we didn't understand something, she'd say, "You know what so-and-so means, don't you?" then proceed to translate or explain it no matter how many times she'd done that before.

Our maternal grandmother continually criticized Dad to us and to our mother, who wasn't exempt from the tongue-lashings she doled out. Grandma Schultz struggled, I always thought, to reconcile herself to the fact that her highly attractive and much sought-after daughter passed over suitors becoming doctors and lawyers to marry a young man she considered something of a country bumpkin, however handsome and brilliant he was and however charming he could be in the right company.

When I entered Fairlington Elementary in September 1947, our school was full, and in time, overflowing. All of my teachers were women. The only male teacher I can remember was one who occasionally visited for physical education.

I had a strong crush on my third grade teacher, Jane Hervy, who was young and pretty. She liked me, too. On the last day of school, she gave me a kiss that made me blush. The guffaw of one of the boys who saw this caused me to run out of the classroom. After a little reflection, my discomfiture turned to pleasure, and it wasn't long before I returned to see my teacher, from whom I wouldn't have minded another kiss. Miss Hervy got married shortly after school ended and moved away, much to my regret. I was also smitten that year by the daughter of our Cub Scout master, a beautiful girl with long hair. Like so many people in our highly transient area, she was gone before I knew it.

Fourth grade was a difficult time for me. For a good part of it, I fancied myself as protecting the class from a strong but somewhat troubled friend, who was having a bad year and negative influence on me as he disrupted our lessons and bullied classmates. In defiance of my teacher's orders, I once stalked him around the classroom in a scene that could have come from *The Blackboard Jungle*. My macho behavior was all the more troubling since my teacher was the mother of two of my neighbors and pals.

Perhaps I had taken an unintended cue from Dad, who had

an air of toughness about him that wasn't just bluff. His accounts of survival training on Catalina Island in preparation for OSS duty, travels in the Far East during World War II, and dangerous missions to Korea, impressed me. When he returned from Korea one time, I told my class how Dad wanted to boot someone he was interrogating "in the ass," and soon heard from Mother that I shouldn't use language like that in school. Dad's good friend and frequent visitor to our house, John Churchill, may also have influenced my persona that year.

John Churchill and my father shared many interests—history, love of hiking, and fondness for women, one of whom was my mother. One time, Dad humiliated Mother in front of Churchill by forcing her do something against her will, exactly what I never learned. She fled to the bedroom in tears and was followed there by our guest, who tried to comfort her. If Mother had let him, he would have done much more than that, which was true of many of Dad's friends over the years.

Churchill called us brothers the "little bastards." He said that with a grin, but there was a hard edge to it as well. A flier during the war, Churchill was shot down behind enemy lines. In the process of escaping, he killed a man in hand-to-hand combat, I once heard. A wound he received deprived him of his sense of taste, but not his appetite, Mother recalled.

On one visit, Churchill brought along a fiery redhead whose beauty matched his own handsomeness. Much to my surprise, she gave me a kiss on the cheek that turned me the color of her hair. While Mother was pregnant with Charlie, she mailed Churchill a message he never received. I remember how she cried when she read the letter and obituary his father sent back, and the sadness I felt thinking of John and his friend skiing high in the Swiss Alps the day a big avalanche buried them.

Thanks to Jessie C. Carpenter, who resided half way between our house and the one Kimberly and her family later occupied, sixth grade was my best year of elementary school. At the beginning of assemblies, plump Miss Carpenter would stand in front of us and raise her hand to command our attention. When this was not forthcoming quickly enough, she would say, "Enough's enough and too much is *naasty*" in her aristocratic Virginia accent. Then we would quiet down. This dedicated and caring lady spoke with fondness of her roots in Berryville, the home of two U.S. senators. Pride in her state and country, however, didn't blind her to their faults, for at the beginning of every school year, she would tell the assembled students, "The darkest day in American history was when the framers of the Constitution failed to abolish slavery."

My fellow students elected me captain of the safety patrols, one of the most prestigious positions in the school. For a while, I fancied myself some sort of commandant whom the patrols on duty should salute as I made my rounds to inspect them. In my academic work, I aimed for perfection, but usually achieved frustration. Miss Carpenter liked me, expressed pride in me, and encouraged me as a leader, which made my self-confidence grow. On my first semester report card, she wrote:

*John has exhibited outstanding ability in being able to assume responsibility and get along with other people. He is an excellent patrol captain and leader in classroom activities.*

Concern for her pupils' social development led Miss Carpenter to teach us the rudiments of dancing, proper table manners, the correct way to seat a lady, and how to meet and address adults. My southern habit of saying "ma'am" and "sir" probably dates to this time. To reinforce these lessons, she organized two sixth grade dances. She also encouraged a sense of independence in us.

When a classmate and I skipped school one morning to catch a bus to Washington for a Senators baseball game at Griffith Stadium, and returned to school in the early afternoon after discovering we'd gone the wrong day, she welcomed us as if we'd done nothing wrong and suggested we draw a picture or write about our experience during the remainder of class.

Memorable field trips we took were to the Washington mosque and the Iranian Embassy, where we saw a big portrait of the Shah, learned about Irans's oil and carpets, and tasted some of its sweets and pistachios. Miss Carpenter expected us to dress up and act maturely on our excursions. Following these visits, we had lunch at the Hot Shoppe, where we were able to practice the good manners she taught us. My mother, to her delight and mine, came along as a chaperon both times.

Toward the end of the year, I developed a crush on a girl in my class named Ginny, who lived down the street from me. After school, I'd walk past her house in the hope of seeing her outside. When that didn't happen, I screwed up my courage and knocked on her door before her father got home from work. The highlight of my brief courtship was getting to kiss her while we stood out of sight along the side of her house. A friend and classmate who often accompanied me on these visits, and with whom I dissected them afterwards, also joined in the kissing. On occasion, even Dick came along to participate in this pleasure.

My fondness for girls extended to two others, who lived only a few doors from each other. When I wasn't off seeing Ginny, I'd visit them in back of their homes, where we sat on a stoop and talked. One of them was my date to the second sixth grade party, but all three girls fought to dance with me that night, the pinnacle of my success with the opposite sex until Kimberly and I became lovers.

At the end of the year, Miss Carpenter wrote my parents:

*John has the highest of standards for himself. As he is a perfectionist—nothing less than the very highest and the product a professional or one highly skilled with long years of training would present seems to give John a depth of satisfaction. This trait is noble and to be commended but I have tried to help John see that even the best had to learn and he is in the process of learning and with the type of effort he puts forth he will achieve success but the type of success he desires just must be in the future. I feel that he has gained understanding of this problem and it is my hope that he has gained sufficient confidence not to be discouraged. He has demonstrated the trait of being very fair-minded. He can't stand seeing someone being misunderstood or not given every advantage. He has assumed responsibility for class activities and has been most dependable. His standards are very high and it is hard when others do not have the same perfection in mind. He still needs help in how to encourage others to reach his principles and standards without becoming discouraged himself. He must continue to be a leader, as well as a follower (which he can do) because of his recognized ability by his classmates. He owes this to his peers and to the world.*

Miss Carpenter ended her assessment with these words:

*I shall always be interested in John's progress and would appreciate hearing from him.*

One of the few regrets I have carried through life is that I visited this exceptional lady only once after I left Fairlington Elementary. When I did, she was principal of the school. In her excitement to see me, she kissed me squarely on the mouth.

The confidence I had in myself as a leader, and in dealing with girls, was far greater at the end of sixth grade than at any other time. Unfortunately, this didn't last long when I started seventh grade in a much larger place.

## 5 Loner

Those of us born shortly before the official start of the baby boom were a large cohort in our own right. In fact, we were numerous enough to necessitate the construction of a new secondary school in south Arlington. Wakefield, ten minutes by bus from my home, opened for grades seven through ten in September 1953 in spite of being only half finished. In time, it became a senior high school for grades ten through twelve.

The three-hour orientation trip we sixth graders from Fairlington took to one of the junior high schools in the county did nothing to prepare me for my new experience. Throughout seventh grade, workmen were all over the school, interrupting classes to connect or finish something. At noon, they congregated outside on the street by the lunch trucks. Occasionally, a friend and I waited in line with them to buy a hot dog and soft drink. Finding my way around this large school took some doing at first, but was less of a problem than no longer being in a familiar and reassuring environment, where I enjoyed a certain prominence and popularity.

Our Wakefield student body was white and American-born. The only foreigners I recall during six years there were twin sisters from Sweden, whose hair was as blond as mine. A number of my seventh grade peers were more mature physically and self-assured socially than I. Dress was one way I sought to combat my insecurities. During the year, I acquired black suede shoes, a pink shirt, black sport coat and tie, and ducktail hair style that helped me stand out sartorially on special occasions.

One of these occasions was the seventh grade dance held in May. To open the dance, Mr. Winkler, my gym teacher and the faculty sponsor of the event, chose me and Bobbi Coulter, on whom I had a crush. Bobbi was pretty, outgoing, and popular, in no way self-conscious like me. Unaware of how the system in these dances worked, I made a mistake that cost me dearly. At the end of our solo, I thought I was supposed to select a boy to dance in my place with a girl Bobbi would choose. "No, no, John," Mr. Winkler said with a smile, "you need to choose a girl!" The laughter my faux pas brought from my peers so embarrassed me that I turned away from further participation in social activities for several years.

In many ways, I felt isolated at Wakefield and was becoming a loner. By the time I got up the courage to go to another social affair, I felt lost watching everyone doing unfamiliar dances, ones I was too inhibited to try, thereby perpetuating my social isolation.

Before seventh grade, I developed a predilection for the company of grown women and a keen appreciation of the female form. During early childhood visits to Trenton, I loved to sit in the breakfast room and listen to the ladies talk while having afternoon coffee and cake. As I followed Papa down the stairs to the basement, with its dark wooden paneling and small windows that let in little light, I entered a different world. My sense of fright soon left me when I sat on the floor next to the stacks of old *Esquire* magazines he'd neatly piled on shelves, and began looking at Vargas drawings of scantily clad, voluptuous women, precursors of *Playboy* pinups.

When Mother's friends came to visit in our Fairlington home, rather than clearing out as my brothers did, I stuck around to see what was going on. Mother used to say "I was all ears." Women seemed to like me, too. Lou Rigg, a neighbor for whose children I sometimes babysat, would say with a big grin that she'd "go for me" if she weren't already married. My affinity for women and their company outweighed that which I had for men. From direct observation and reading, I knew women were often mistreated and taken advantage of, even when doing their best to please us self-centered males.

Besides baseball cards, I collected "wolf cards" during the height of their popularity in the early 1950s. These were playing cards with color photographs of naked women on one side and the drawing of a leering wolf on the other. Dick, and even Steve, joined me in this endeavor. We bought the cards at Al's Magic Shop in Washington and traded them with each other and a few of our friends. By today's standards, they were chaste, but to us, they were alluring. We never had large numbers of them, as we did of baseball cards, for far fewer were available, and they cost much more. We were also choosy about what we acquired and kept, since we didn't find all the women featured on them equally attractive.

Cards that shocked me were the black and white "army cards" I saw in the boys' room at Wakefield late in the seventh grade and beginning of eighth. These depicted soldiers in Europe lined up to gawk at, or fondle, women who attempted to show their starved audience as much of their anatomy as possible. The first time I saw them, I brooded about them on the school bus all the way home.

Following my youngest brother's birth, my parents moved from their small upstairs bedroom to the downstairs room we played in, thus giving me a room of my own. I now had privacy and a place to retreat during times when Dad was at his worst. On such occasions, I often fantasized about "killing the bastard" when I got older. To characterize his behavior, I gradually thought up different names for him, such as "Theodorsky" and the "Terrible T," suggestive of a mad Russian tsar, as well as "Thor," the Norse god of thunder.

A classic image of Jesus that sat on a hanging shelf along with my collections of civil war bullets and Indian arrow heads comforted me. Using savings from my paper route, I bought a cherry desk to study at. Above it, I hung a famous picture of a nude Marilyn Monroe taken while she was still Norma Jean Baker. One afternoon, a five-year-old neighbor Mother cared for while his parents worked wandered into my room as I was studying at my desk. Staring at the picture on the wall, he exclaimed, "Boy, she sure has big muscles!"

On Friday and Saturday nights, I lay in bed until early in the morning listening to an Arlington DJ, who was one of the first in our area to play the new rock and roll music coming out. On Sunday mornings, I often listened to gospel singing broadcast from black churches in Washington.

Prior to puberty, I had few inhibitions, and frequently wandered around the house without any clothes. Early one morning, when I was seven, I happened to be sitting in the middle of the kitchen floor naked when a neighbor and playmate came to the back door to borrow some sugar. She knocked, and looked through the window. As startled as I was, she ran home with an empty cup while I jumped up and fled into the living room.

With the appearance of hair in new places, a changing voice, and signs of a prominent Adam's apple on my long neck, I no longer felt comfortable appearing in the buff in front of my parents or even Dick or Steve. The growth this mysterious process brought impressed my prepubescent brothers whenever they happened to spy it. Once, Dick blurted out, "Boy, you've got big balls!" I was proud of being bigger, but that was compared to what I'd been, not to most of my peers who stood next to me naked in the shower room at school. Happily, the effect of this growth became more obvious when stiffness set in.

A variety of stimuli—thoughts, pictures, smells, memories, or touch—can bring on a youthful erection, or merely the time of day, when it can happen with some regularity or by surprise, most awkwardly, in the middle of class when one might be called to the blackboard. When I had one in my room, I discovered I could make myself flap up and down. Once, young Charlie wandered in when I was sitting on the bed doing this. I said "woo woo" as he watched and laughed. A day or two later, I made the same sound at the dinner table. To my great surprise and chagrin, Charlie piped up, "That's the sound Johnny made when he showed me his peenie."

As my gonads fired up, stranger things began to happen. The first incident was the most shocking. Awakening with a sudden start early one morning, I found the underpants I slept in wet, slippery, and pungent in odor. Hoping my mother wouldn't notice when she did the wash, I blotted my briefs and soiled sheets with tissue paper. As fresh as my semen was the memory of my dream, an eerie encounter with Mother. Thereafter, these unsettling experiences came periodically, sometimes with different actors. The day my own hand would control my emissions was still far off.

I didn't have much in the way of formal religious education until the fifth or sixth grade. In fact, I wasn't even baptized until January 2, 1949. On that day, at Grandma Wertime's behest, a family friend and minister who taught at a nearby college, came to her house when a number of her grandchildren were there over the New Year's holiday, lined us all up, and to our good grandmother's satisfaction, sprinkled some water on our heads to enable our salvation.

Until I went to Sunday school, my ideas about religion were based mainly on Bible stories Mother read to us and various unorthodox explanations she gave when we asked her questions. Mother had a strong spiritual bent and was firm in her faith, but somewhat fuzzy in her theology. She considered herself a Protestant, and subscribed to basic tenants of the Christian faith, such as the idea of eternal bliss in heaven, from which she excluded nobody. What really captivated her, however, was the idea of reincarnation and the prospect of communicating with the dead, which she'd heard about listening to the radio in her youth.

For about five years, Mother sang in the choir of the Fair-Park Baptist Church. Her close friends, Kitty and Lou, were choir members, and she happily joined them. Mother's choir career more or less coincided with the ministry of the Reverend Grady Hutchinson, Jr., a warm, outgoing man who took his pastoral work seriously. Among the many people he visited was Kitty's cancer-stricken mother from North Carolina, who spent the last months of her life in a small bedroom across from our house.

At my mother's urging and from my own need at the time for some kind of spiritual connection, I attended Sunday school at Fair-Park Baptist for about a year, and afterward, sometimes went to the eleven o'clock church service there. Sitting in the congregation by myself, I watched my mother in her light blue robe sing with the choir and as a soloist, something she alone in our family could do.

The Southern Baptists, I discovered, had a stricter code of behavior and a more conservative view of race, women, and other denominations than I liked. My Sunday school attendance at Fair-Park Baptist ceased well before Mother herself abandoned that church shortly after Reverend Hutchinson was ousted as pastor. Among other things, he was accused of ministering to people who weren't Fair-Park members, like our neighbor's dying mother. During Mother's years in the choir, Dad complained that her Sunday morning singing and weekly practice interfered with his own schedule and needs. Now he was free of these inconveniences.

When I was thirteen and staying at Grandma Wertime's for a couple of weeks during the summer, my grandmother took me to Sunday school at her Presbyterian Church. Dad went there while growing up, learned the Bible well, and won many prizes, but never said a word to me about religion, pro or con. The stern lady who taught us assigned me two psalms to memorize for the following Sunday, but I didn't get around to doing it. In class the next week, she roundly chastised me for my sloth.

"I didn't have a Bible," I pleaded.

"Don't tell me you couldn't find a Bible in Mrs. Wertime's house!" she said tartly. "I know better than that!" I knew better, too, and never attended another Sunday school class in my life.

A year or so later, the oldest of our surrogate sisters wanted to take me back to Fair-Park Baptist. She had a Sunday school assignment to bring in a sinner in need of salvation, and asked my mother if I'd be willing to go along. Her invitation both touched and amused me, but I declined.

Aware that I had no social interaction with my female peers, Dad used to advise me that "the best place to meet girls is in church, where they feel safe." With this in mind, I went with Scotty Strother, my classmate and friend from grade school days, to a Sunday night youth group program at Fairlington Presbyterian, but nothing came of it.

Most Saturday mornings when we didn't have baseball games, Dad would announce he was leaving for Pennsylvania and that anyone going should get ready immediately. Until the age of thirteen, I went along. After that, I often stayed home. It wasn't because I had something better to do in Fairlington. I just needed to be apart from the family, especially my father. While they were gone, time would pass slowly, creating a loneliness and sadness that nearly brought tears to my eyes.

Sunday mornings were the worst part of the weekend, a time when I'd stand out on our playing field along Quaker Lane and watch adults and their children happily enter and leave St. Clement's. This sight created a sense of emptiness in me I couldn't dispel. Something significant should fill that special time of the week, I thought to myself. Those I watched seemed to have found it. I longed for it, too, but couldn't attain it alone. When Kimberly and I became companions and lovers, all that changed.

Just before the beginning of ninth grade, I was excited to learn that a new gym teacher and basketball coach at Wakefield had moved into the deep court adjacent to mine. I saw him a time or two outside his first floor apartment before I got up the courage to introduce myself. "Coach," as he told me to call him, had played guard in college. He was a quiet man, who could sometimes appear pensive or moody. He seemed to like me. In my youthful fervor, I came to idolized him the way I did Ted Williams.

During the first few months of school, I sporadically bumped into Coach at Wakefield or in our neighborhood. Once basketball season started, our meetings became more frequent, especially in the locker room or on the court. He ran the the high school junior varsity team while I played on the junior high varsity. Whenever I could, I got a ride home with Coach, which gave us an opportunity to chat. On one occasion, I visited him briefly in his home and met his wife and infant daughter.

At a practice session over the Christmas vacation when his team and mine were sharing the gym, Coach told me his family was away, and asked if I'd like to spend New Year's Eve with him. Delighted to be invited, I showed up at his home around nine.

Sitting side by side on his sofa, we watched television and had some ice cream. One of the acts on TV that night was a rock and roll band I enjoyed immensely, but which he found odd. He laughed heartily when I told him how great the group was. The divide in our taste in music and dance was a gaping one, as big as it was with my parents' generation.

As soon as auld lang syne had been sung, Coach turned off the TV. "John," he said, "it's late. You're welcome to spend the night, or if you like, go home." I decided to stay, and followed him into the bedroom of his small apartment, where I found only a double bed. Coach changed into his pajamas, and indicated I could sleep in my underwear next to him. I was a bit surprised at this arrangement, but didn't hesitate because of the high regard in which I held him.

With our long frames, the bed was a tight fit for the two of us. Coach asked which side I'd like, and I chose the left, next to the bathroom, which I usually had to visit during the night. Around seven-thirty, the sun was up, but I was still tired from a fitful sleep and not fully awake. As I lay on my back, I suddenly sensed something move next to me, then felt Coach's hand on my abdomen, caressing me. This went on for about a minute until I became uncomfortably aroused and embarrassed. Turning over quickly onto my stomach, as if shifting my position in the middle of a sound sleep, I remained motionless, awaiting an opportunity to get up and get dressed without being seen. That finally came when Coach went into the bathroom and shut the door. By the time he came out, I was fully clothed and ready to go home for breakfast.

The import of this incident didn't register on me, so great was my innocence and trust. Two years would pass before it did, and then only when Coach himself made an oblique allusion to it during an unusual conversation we had on the basketball court.

## 6  Babysitter

The first time I babysat for Kimberly's girls was a Friday night in late September. I arrived a few minutes before seven in order to become acquainted with them before Kimberly's date showed up. Both girls seemed happy to see me. Jill was in the fourth grade. Like her mother, she was tall with long facial features, but had larger, sadder, more oval-shaped eyes. Martie was in the second grade. Of a shorter build than her sister, she had a pixie face with freckles and a quick, engaging smile. Before they went upstairs to their room, Kimberly gave us instructions about snacks and bedtime, then kissed them good night.

Ten minutes later, we heard a knock at the door. Standing there was Reverend Hopson, wearing a sport coat and tie.

"Maurice, right on time as usual!" Kimberly quipped with a smile.

Mother's boss countered with feigned surprise, "Am I late?"

"Have you met Peggy's son, Johnny?" Kim asked.

"Yes, of course," he replied. "It's good to see you again, Johnny."

"Thank you, sir, it's good to see you, too," I said.

Kimberly looked happy to see the parson. He helped her with her coat, and as they were on the way out, she shouted up the stairs, "Bye Jillilee, bye Martiegirl. Be good for Johnny!" Then she turned and said, "I'll be back by ten, Johnny. Thanks for coming."

I was planning to do some homework during my first sit for the Blake girls, but before starting, I looked around a bit. Kim's home was neat, cheerful, and tastefully decorated. Her Fairlington unit, like ours, shared a porch and a wall with the neighbor on the right, and a wall only with the one on the left, but was smaller than the one we lived in. To the left of the door, in front of the drapes covering the two front windows and wall, was a small table with a lamp. Next to that, Kimberly had placed a chair, a dried flower arrangement, and an enormous antique copper kettle filled with magazines and newspapers. A sofa, standing lamp, and two small chairs occupied the left side of the living room. On the right, a baby grand piano filled the space leading up to the second floor. Carpeting on the wooden floor and stairs absorbed the noise I was used to hearing at home and, with the coming of colder weather, provided a welcome warmth.

When I passed through the small dining room into the kitchen to get a drink, everything was in place. I noticed how the electric stove shone without the encrusted burner rings so familiar at home. A sideboard stood in front of the dining room window, which looked out on the large common lawn and playground in back. Chimes hung from a bookcase separating the dining room from the living room. Throughout the house, Kimberly had arranged various objects to good effect, including a sizable painting of a floral arrangement on her dining room wall.

Other than the faint sound of a television coming from the big upstairs bedroom where Kim, Jill, and Martie slept, the house was silent. No one clomped around, practiced the piano, violin, or viola, played the radio or record player, bounced a ball, or bellowed "Peg" or "Mom." Sitting on Kimberly's living room couch, I felt at home and at ease.

After reading a while, I went up to check on the girls. They were dressed in pajamas and lounged on their beds, with their chins resting on delicately folded hands. When I knocked on the open door, they jumped up and smiled. "I wanted to see if everything's okay," I said. "Your mom mentioned you can have a snack before bed. If you have one, I'll join you."

Following our chat over cookies and milk, I scrapped my plans to study and watched television with them instead. Time flew by. During a commercial, I noticed the clock. There was just enough time to brush teeth and turn off the light.

Kimberly came home promptly at ten. She asked how things had gone, paid me, and thanked me for coming. From the small closet opposite the front door, she handed me my dark green corduroy jacket with the name Wakefield emblazoned in white. "Johnny, it's starting to rain" she said. "I'll run you home." I thanked her, but declined the offer, knowing I could jog there almost as fast as it would take to go by car.

When I got home from school Monday afternoon, Mother was

waiting to tell me something. "Kimberly came by the office this morning singing your praises," she said. "Jill and Martie loved you, and hope you'll come back to sit for them again!" I was happy their reaction was favorable. It was an easy sit, the money was good, I liked Kimberly's girls, and even more, Kimberly herself. Unlike my own home, theirs was a place where I could truly relax.

Fall was the best season of the year for me. Being back in school with homework to do, afternoon pickup basketball on the outdoor court at Fairlington School, touch football in one of the neighboring courts, my paper route, and now, a babysitting job, time passed much more quickly than it had during the languid summer. Gradually, the air got cooler and crisper. Soon it was the end of October.

Like the other children in Fairlington, I had always looked forward to Halloween. By tenth grade, however, I didn't feel comfortable trick-or-treating any longer, so I stayed home to hand out candy while Mother took Charlie out and Dick and Steve made their rounds. About seven-thirty, two fully costumed kids appeared at the door. Both were giggling, then one shouted, "Trick or treat." As I offered them candy, the other one said, "Hi, Johnny!" Looking closer, I recognized Jill and Martie. Off in the distance stood Kimberly, wearing a high conical hat. "Happy Halloween from an old witch!" she exclaimed, waving her arm as if it were a wand. They thanked me and were off.

My growing crush on Kimberly and her girls led me to walk by their house in the hope of seeing them out in front by their green Ford station wagon parked on the street, or at play in the big court in back. Giddy at the thought of them, I couldn't help myself. It was as if they had cast a spell on me.

In order to get a high school teaching job, Kimberly was taking night classes towards a B.A. in history at American University in Washington. My regular babysitting made it possible for her to study again, she said. She also told my mother how much they all liked me, and how handsome I was. I, in turn, thought about Kimberly and her girls constantly.

It didn't take long to get used to one another's company. Soon, we seemed almost like a family. For fun, the four of us sometimes visited Gifford's Ice Cream Parlor, where three scoops with hot fudge cost forty-five cents. Lean and physically fit, I had no trouble wolfing down a big dish like this. In fact, my appetite was legendary among my family members, one of whom dubbed me "the vacuum cleaner," and another, "the typewriter" when I ate corn on the cob.

The Centre Theater next to the Blessed Sacrament Church and School basketball court, where I often played, was a place those of us in Fairlington frequented. Once in a while, I took Jill and Martie there in the evening when Kim went out on a weekend date. Occasionally, Kimberly, the girls, and I went together. Looking at me with a big grin, she would sometimes refer to herself and her girls as my "three females," or say, "Well, Johnny, how does it feel to have three females to look after?" I was very happy to think of myself as their protector. My attachment to them helped me quickly overcome the pain of rejection by Phillips Exeter.

Christmastime was especially pleasant at the home of the mother and daughters I'd come to adore. They put up a big tree, trimmed it beautifully, tied stockings, wreaths, and bows to the bannister along the staircase, and hung mistletoe at the entrance to the living room. Planting herself under it when I came in to sit one night, Kimberly called out to me impishly, "Johnny, look where I'm standing!" I blushed a bit, but gave her a little peck on the cheek. "Come on," she said, "you can do better than that!" This time, I got a quick taste of her full red lips. I wouldn't have minded even more than that, but she was out of reach, a woman almost my mother's age who was in love with Reverend Hopson.

When my JV basketball games weren't too far away, Kimberly and her girls came to watch. The first game they attended took place on a cold Friday night in mid-January at Hammond High School in Alexandria. My teammates and I were on the court warming up when they came in and sat down in the middle of the bleachers on the visitor's side. Jill and Martie were the youngest ones there; Kimberly was the most striking and sophisticated. Whenever I ran past them, my own cheering squad shouted out, "Yeah, Johnny" or "Go Johnny, go."

I played a lot that game, and our strong team defeated the Admirals. After I dressed and came out of the locker room, my fans were waiting for me. Kimberly congratulated us on our victory, and remarked with a smile how much she and the girls enjoyed "watching me lope up and down the court." Then she asked, "Would you like to ride home with us, Johnny?" By that time, most of the team was milling around in the lobby, waiting for Coach to appear. When he did, I approached him, pointed to Kim, and said, "My mother's friend and her girls came to watch the game. They live in Fairlington. May I get a ride home with them?" Thinking nothing of it, Coach replied, "Sure. Go ahead." Offering me the keys, Kimberly grinned and said, "You're welcome to drive us, Johnny."

As we got into the car at the rear of the parking lot, I spotted my teammates boarding the Wakefield bus. When it began to roll, I pulled along side it in order to pass. At that moment, I looked up and saw at every windowpane a teammate's face looking down at us.

During basketball practice the following Monday, Scotty, my teammate and longtime buddy, sided up to me and said with an awestruck kind of laughter, "Who's that woman of yours I saw in the car after the Hammond game? For someone who never goes out on a date, it seems you're doing pretty well for yourself!" Tickled at the thought and by his boldness, I joined him in a hearty laugh, but soon set the record straight, saying, "She's my mother's best friend, and those are her daughters I babysit."

Deep inside me I felt an emptiness and yearning for someone to hold and to love. I was intoxicated by the sound of Kimberly's voice and the image of her it conjured up in my brain. Yet it didn't occur to me that Kimberly could ever be "my woman."

Academically, tenth grade went along well enough, but I shouldn't have taken mechanical drawing. Mr. Scartz, my teacher, thought highly of me, not for any talent I had in his class, but because he liked me as a person. I got through the course with a B instead of the D I deserved, thanks to this and the help of a future naval architect who sat next to me.

As in previous years, my grade socially was F, but my JV baseball season as catcher under Lefty Freisem, my all-time favorite coach, was more successful. In one game, I hit three home runs, and in another, four.

Throughout the year that Mother worked as church secretary, she often mentioned Kimberly's desire to wed Mr. Hopson, as well as the increasing frustration Kimberly felt at her lack of success. During my sitting jobs, I could see the efforts she made. According to what my mother once told me, Kimberly's relationship with Mr. Hopson almost got tripped up by money she thought she had loaned him, but which he interpreted to be "a gift to the parson." They straightened this out, but the basic question of his interest in her was still unresolved.

Becoming increasingly despondent, Kimberly bought a book on self-hypnosis and attempted to dispel her feelings for her reluctant suitor. As she sat on the bed in the small back bedroom she used as a den and office, Kimberly demonstrated to Mother the methods she'd learned from the book. Hearing about this alarmed me, for I wanted Kimberly and her girls to be happy in life. In my thoughts and prayers, I fervently hoped Kimberly would reach her goal of marrying Mr. Hopson. However, when she pressed him on this subject, Mr. Hopson replied, "You know, Kim, sometimes the chemistry just isn't right." The meaning of this, she told me years later, clicked in her mind when she happened to see a photograph of three handsome young men on a table in his bedroom. Then she realized he wasn't one of the marrying kind.

A time or two, Dad expressed interest in having some Persian rugs to help spruce up our home. When Mother saw a full page ad in the *Washington Post* with pictures and prices of rugs on sale at Sloan's in Washington, I heard her exclaim, "Oh goody! I'll call Kimberly to see if she wants to go with me." Kimberly had the same idea, so off they went in search of woven treasure. Late that afternoon, my mother came back with a dining room carpet, a runner, two mats, and a small throw rug. At the time, they seemed wonderful, and they certainly added color and interest to the house. Kimberly, on the other hand, spent her money on a single, better quality piece, which she put in her dining room.

These first rugs I lived with must have worked a special magic on me. Some years later, during my long sojourn in Iran, I became a collector and connoisseur of woven art, and later, an internationally known writer and dealer in the field of antique rugs and textiles.

On April 9, 1957, my family celebrated my sixteenth birthday.

Nine days later came Kimberly's thirty-fourth. Before long, school was out and it was summer. At the end of June, shortly before they were to go off to a camp Kimberly directed, Mother invited the Blakes to come to the "Mountain Place," where the Wertime clan was having a get-together.

## 7 The Mountain Place

The car my parents purchased in 1951 gave Dad the means to roam and explore in the western part of Northern Virginia, Maryland, and south central Pennsylvania, where he was born and grew up. Eager to have a place he, we, and all the Wertimes could use for weekend getaways, holidays, and summer vacations, in 1952 my father urged his mother and siblings who didn't live far away, to band together with him to buy sixty acres of forested land on the side of a small mountain near Fort Loudon. The property contained two houses, a garage, a few outbuildings, and a small stream, close to which we built a pond for swimming and fishing.

The Wertime family was a remarkably cordial, cohesive, and caring one during my childhood and beyond, to the credit of its gentle but tough matriarch, Flora Wertime. Possessing a keen mind, excellent memory, and strong Protestant faith, she attended college for two years before dropping out to marry her music professor and start a family. The Latin she'd learned came in handy in helping her six children with their lessons. All of them went to college, and five of them obtained higher degrees. Joe, the baby of the family, entered the steel industry after graduation. Later, he owned several small businesses.

At the Mountain Place, my brothers and I soon remembered, or quickly discovered, that we were part of a family addicted to work. When one member toiled, anyone close by was expected to pitch in, whether or not it was convenient or welcomed. This attitude likely stemmed from our grandmother's upbringing on a West Virginia farm and the difficult times of the Great Depression, when all the children had to help their widowed mother keep the family afloat. Our father, it was clear to me, was the most tireless worker in the family apart from his mother.

Our new property, with its myriad problems, gave Dad the perfect outlet to satisfy his need for strenuous physical labor. Every morning after breakfast, he'd say to Mother, "Where're the boys? Tell'em it's time to work!" Mother would dutifully come and report what Dad had said. We'd all groan, "Oh no! Not again!" then, traipse outside to do his bidding. In this manner, my brothers and I spent many a summer vacation at the Mountain Place working from just after breakfast till mid-afternoon.

Our job was to clean up the trash the former owners had thrown onto a huge heap above the "Upper House"—a somewhat dark and dreary old hunting lodge—or had stored in its attic over a period of fifty years. Once a week, Uncle Joe came in his dump truck, which we and any of our cousins he brought along or happened to be around, would fill with old bottles, tin cans, newspapers, worn-out furniture, and other junk. When we weren't doing that, we helped Dad build something or repair a roof, clear brush, mow the lawns, paint, and whatever else he could think of. We came to hate this constant grind, but had no choice in the matter.

When the work day ended around three, we amused ourselves with swimming and fishing in the pond, hiking, throwing horse shoes, playing catch, badminton, or baseball with a pingpong ball. We also smoked dried seed pod "stogies" from the catalpa tree in front of the Upper House or dried corn silk in our corn cob pipes *à la* Tom Sawyer and Huckleberry Finn, things Dad had taught us to do. Eating fresh peaches and apples from the local orchards and reading the latest comic books, especial *Mad*, which I considered one of the funniest things ever published, rounded out our usual diversions. Mother's good cooking and the wonderful tomatoes and corn abundant in August went a long way to assuage our fatigue.

To break the routine, we sometimes rode to a state park to swim in the lake, take a hike up the mountainside, or drive to a nearby town for a milkshake in the evening. Shopping for candy and comic books and observing the people in an old-time country store was always fun. The sound of Harry Kieffer, the owner, saying "aaw yeh-yuh" in answer to a question or as an exclamation, will always be with me.

At our family retreat, I had the only hunting experience of my life. On a warm summer day, I set out into the forest above the Upper

House with my BB gun. I didn't have a particular prey in mind, so when I spotted a large frog sunning itself by the brook, I took aim and shot it. Pride in my marksmanship turned to regret as soon as I saw the innocent creature lying there dead. After this wanton act, I lost any desire to take a life, except for those of the gnats and mosquitoes that thrived in the swampy grounds below the old hunting lodge where my family and I ate and slept.

On the last Saturday in June, I drove the Blakes in their station wagon up to our mountain home for a Wertime family gathering. As we reached the end of the narrow lane that led from the highway to the open area in which the Lower House, a two-hundred-year-old log cabin, stood next to our pond, we saw Dick and Steve by the water with a number of our cousins and an aunt, who was a pediatrician. Not far away was her husband, a dentist and Irish Catholic. Another aunt was also there with her young daughters and music professor spouse. Along the short winding stretch leading from the pond to the Upper House there were more relatives, including Dad's cousin from Wheeling, West Virginia, and, my cousin, Franny. As we approached the house, still others came into view, some playing badminton or throwing horse shoes. Jill and Martie looked overwhelmed by the large crowd. Someone shouted to Mother that we'd arrived, and she rushed out to greet us with Charlie at her side.

"My God, Johnny," Kim whispered as we were getting out of the car, "are there any Wertimes who aren't here today?" Happy to see someone they knew, Kimberly, Jill, and Martie gave my mother and youngest brother a big hug. Dad soon appeared in the old swimming suit he wore while he was working. He greeted Kimberly and the girls as Grandma Schultz came up from behind and said, "Hi ya, Kim, hi ya kids!" Kimberly turned and answered in surprise, "Well, hello, Irma, I didn't know we'd see you here today."

Following the deaths of my grandfather and great-grandmother within a few months of each other in late 1956, Grandma Schultz left California and moved into a house in Fairlington, not far from where Kimberly lived. While out on a walk with her dog or shopping just across from Fairlington at Bradlee, she sometimes bumped into Kimberly and her girls. Kimberly enjoyed my grandmother's feistiness, off-color language, and sense of humor. From time to time, she  dropped by to visit her.

To work up an appetite at these family affairs, most of us went swimming before eating. On some occasions we had our picnic lunch down by the pond. The day Kim and her girls came to visit, the ladies of the family laid our meal out in the old hunting lodge, on long narrow tables filling the enclosed side porch, and on a picnic table sitting on the porch in front.

By the time we had swum, dried off, and changed, everyone who was coming had arrived. Mother introduced Kimberly, Jill, and Martie to all they hadn't met, and I tried to help them feel at home as much as possible.

From the moment we reached the Mountain Place, Kim created quite a stir. The long pony tail streaming down her back toward her rounded buttocks and long ballerina legs distinguished our tall, graceful visitor from the rest of the women, as did her natural flair with words, gesture, and ready laughter. Before heeding the call to lunch, I saw a number of my uncles, all eager to flirt, gather around Kim on the side lawn close to the front porch as a couple of eagle-eyed aunts observed from a distance.

Two uncles were particularly attentive and affable that day. In fact, they almost slobbered over our guest. The aunts who were watching, I quickly sensed, weren't at all pleased. Furthermore, Kimberly was a person who had to touch while talking, which meant her hands were always busy grasping or lightly caressing whomever she happened to be addressing. I'd often experienced this habit of hers, and understood the subtle but powerful effect it had on a man. Witnessing a scene so unusual for a Wertime gathering, I, too, was no less moved by Kimberly's beauty and charm. In truth, I worshiped her and longed to have someone like her for my own. My greatest hope was for her happiness and successful marriage to Reverend Hopson.

At the end of a long day of swimming, eating, playing, and conversing, I drove three tired Blakes home to Fairlington. In a couple of days, they'd be leaving for a six week long summer camp at a church retreat. On their return, Kimberly told me, she would call me for more babysitting. I said goodbye to them, walked home, and went to bed, as I, too, was fatigued from the full day we had enjoyed.

In the ninth grade, I developed a strong interest in Princeton University, and was eager to visit the campus and town. With my Ivy League look of buttondown shirts, khaki pants, and saddle shoes, sartorially I would have fit in there very well. I also had a solid academic record. Princeton was about four-and-a-half hours from the Mountain Place, farther by a good bit than the outings we normally took. Dad knew how much I wanted to see the Princeton campus, and that my mother and brothers were willing, so one morning he announced he'd be leaving for Princeton in fifteen minutes and that anyone who wanted to go should get ready immediately. We all scurried around, then piled into our station wagon.

As the oldest son and the one with the longest legs, I always got to ride shotgun. A smaller person sat between Dad and me, and three more on the back seat or in the rear. Our father, although a good driver, had his idiosyncrasies. Our first two cars didn't have an outside mirror on the passenger's side, so it was difficult for Dad to see any cars on our right. Whenever he had to look that way, he'd call out, "Duck your heads!" This habit had become so ingrained that even when a car had a side view mirror, he still said that. Anyone slow in reacting nearly got his head taken off by his dirty looks and angry roars.

Sometimes, when my brothers and I went to the rear of the wagon to relax, play cards, or chat, our father became irritated and exclaimed, "There's too much weight in the back!" When this happened, I'd quip, "Dad's afraid the car'll get tired." We'd all laugh and someone would move forward.

Grandma Schultz was sitting next to Mother on the back seat when Dad once shouted that out. Not having heard this one before, our plump grandmother thought he was referring to her, and took great offense. It took a while for Mother to calm her down, but she finally succeeded, saying, "Ted wasn't referring to you, Mother. He was talking to the boys." Grandma knew Dad's peculiarities well. When criticizing him, she often made a gesture of circles in the air beside her head to indicate he was crazy, or would say, "That father of yours is a little half past six!" with the same meaning.

Traveling down the Pennsylvania Turnpike to New Jersey's main toll road, we reached Princeton in a little over four hours. For a trip of this length with our father, things had gone remarkably well, but we were tired and ready for a break. On Nassau Street, Dad found a parking place right in front of Nassau Hall, the oldest building on campus. On the other side of the street was The English Shop, an Ivy Leaguer's clothing Mecca. Just as I spotted both places, Dad made his announcement, "You've got ten minutes here." My brothers and I looked at one another, then at Mother and Dad. "Ten minutes!" we exclaimed. "That's hardly time enough to pee!" With his strong jaw thrust forward in a determined look, our father replied, "The trip was a long one. I want to get back before it gets dark!" Dad was the driver and the boss. Our visit to Princeton that day lasted little more than a quarter-hour.

Lying in bed in the Upper House early in the morning at the beginning of September, my brothers asleep around me, I could see the sun shining through the trees and hear the whistling wind rustle the changing leaves. Our vacation would soon be at an end, with a new school year about to begin. This transition from summer to fall caused my mood to fluctuate between melancholic and euphoric. Few things in my life were so deliciously bittersweet.

Departing from the Mountain Place, however, bordered on the traumatic. Dad would yell at Mother for not having packed up the clothes, cleaned out the refrigerator, or washed up the utensils and put them away so we could be off at precisely the moment he wanted. Hearing "Come on, Peg, it's time to go" or various words of abuse, Mother would reply, "Hold your horses, Ted. I'm working as fast as I can," or begin to cry.

During such an episode, Uncle Joe became so angry at Dad's demeanor that he wanted to beat him up on the spot. He controlled himself, but reported the incident to Grandma Wertime, who became incensed as well. She wrote Dad a letter in which she thoroughly chastised him for his treatment of Mother, and told him she could "still knock his block off." When the letter arrived in the mail, Dad was at work. Mother opened it, believing it was also intended for her. Shocked at Grandma's scathing message, and wanting to protect our father from his mother's wrath, she tore it up. Dad never had a clue about this letter

55

*Innocence*

and its stern reprimand from a mother he greatly loved and respected.

## 8 New Home

Our Fairlington home was a tight fit when there were five of us, and even more so when we were six. In the hope of remedying the situation, my parents put a deposit on a house under construction in south Arlington, but the builder went bankrupt and they were lucky to get most of their deposit money back. A year later, in August 1957, Mother saw an ad for new houses in an area of north Arlington close to Seven Corners. The property being developed was an old dairy farm. Its former owner, Nelson Reeves, the last to raise milk cows in Arlington, retained the old family house and two-and-a-half acres at the top of a small hill.

Of the many houses Mother saw that month, the best we could afford was a split level on an end lot by the lane running up to the Reeves' home. The house also overlooked a park and the athletic facilities Arlington County was in the process of building. Down the street, other homes were under construction or being laid out. Within a week of seeing it, my parents bought this well-situated house.

At the time of purchase, my brothers and I had been back in school for three weeks, I as a junior, Dick a sophomore, and Steve in the 8th grade. Very conveniently, the new house was in the same school district as Fairlington. I was excited by the prospect of a home with more room, but had reservations about leaving the community I'd lived in for almost eleven of my sixteen years. More importantly, I was alarmed at the prospect of being farther away from Kimberly and her girls and the refuge they provided me, for without a car, I wouldn't be able to get myself back and forth to babysit and see them.

When I went to sit at Kimberly's, she knew what my parents had done and of my concern, but was unperturbed. "Don't worry, Johnny," she said. "There's more than one way to skin a cat. When I need you to sit, I'll come and pick you up and you can spend the night on the bed in the den. When you're ready to go home, I'll take you back on Sunday afternoon, or you can stay and catch the school bus to Wakefield Monday morning. Peggy said this is okay with her if it is with you." Kim's determination to find a way to have me continue to babysit reassured and pleased me.

The day of our move came quickly. To lend moral support to us that late September Saturday morning, Uncle Joe and Aunt Vee came with our four cousins and Grandma Wertime in tow. They brought food for lunch and were ready to help, but the movers wanted everyone out of the way.

Shortly after our move, Kimberly called up to find out how we were doing. Talking to her on the telephone from north Arlington seemed strange at first, but that sensation quickly passed.

It didn't take us long to realize that the three bedrooms of our new home weren't enough. To finish the rec room with separate quarters for Dick and Steve, our father borrowed $9,000 from his mother and hired Fred Rowland, one of the carpenters who'd built our house, to work in the evening. A native of West Virginia, Fred had fast hands and a penchant for talking. I saw a lot of him the following summer when I had a construction job down the street from our home. He was fascinating in his way, but I never really liked him. The initial turmoil and confusion we experienced on North Fourth Road put us under even more stress than we were used to, especially until Fred finished his work downstairs.

Immediately after we moved into our new house, Dad started to landscape the yard. With a young tree he'd dug up in Pennsylvania or closer by hanging out the back of the station wagon, he would pull up in front of the house and expect us to drop whatever we were doing and rush out to help transplant it. When he needed a load of dirt, one of us would have to fetch it from the unfinished park below our house, no matter the time of day or night. Thanks to these efforts, we had the best trees in the neighborhood. Our willingness to help Dad wasn't an issue. It was the timing of his requests and the way he made them that drove us crazy.

Throughout this transition, Mother continued to type at the same pace as before. Dad was working on his first book; Mother's efforts made his scholarship possible.

In early November, when Kimberly called me again for a Saturday night sit, basketball practice had recently started up and my school workload was getting heavier. We agreed she would pick me up at six-thirty, right after dinner. Among Kim's virtues was punctuality, so I had my school books, fresh clothes, and toilet articles ready to go well before she arrived. While Jill and Martie waited in the car, Kim came to the front door to fetch me. Pressed for time and having visited our new home with her daughters a week earlier, Kimberly said, "Peggy, I'd love to stay and chat, but Maurice is coming for me at seven. We've got to get right back."

I was relieved to see Kimberly and the kids once more. "How've you all been?" I asked as I entered the car, and got caught up on their recent activities. This first trip of ours to Fairlington took a little less than twenty minutes, which left Kim just enough time to freshen up for Mr. Hopson.

Much to her surprise and mine, the parson didn't show up that evening as scheduled, but called later to apologize and say there'd been an emergency requiring his presence. That Saturday evening, we all watched TV together in the front bedroom. When it was time to turn in, Kimberly gave me towels, a wash cloth, and a drinking glass. The bed in the den was freshly made up, and I was ready for my first overnight stay with the Blakes.

Sunday morning breakfast was almost ready when I came down around eight. Kimberly was in the kitchen scrambling eggs. Martie was up and dressed, but Jill was still in her pajamas. Kimberly rang the chimes, then called up the stairs, "Jillilee, Martiegirl, time for breakfast." The girls weren't big eaters that morning, which left me enough for seconds and thirds. I joined Kimberly and the girls in clearing off the table, and offered to assist with the dishes, but Kim was too well organized and quick to need any help. Besides, she said, "The kitchen's too small for the two of us with our long arms and legs."

After the dishes were done, Kimberly set the table for lunch, and went upstairs to get herself and her daughters ready for church. While they were gone, I read the newspaper and did some homework up in the den. At twelve forty-five, I heard the door open and someone run up the stairs. Martie had to use the bathroom, which was right at the top, next to the room I was in. Then Jill came up, followed by her mother. "How was church?" I asked. "We didn't go to church," one of the girls said. "We went to Sunday school." During tea time after the service, Kimberly told me, Mr. Hopson took her aside to explain that a parishoner's husband had died, and he had to go to comfort her.

The lamb Kimberly put in the oven before leaving for church was almost done now. Having changed out of her Sunday clothes, she was busy preparing the rest of our dinner when I came into the kitchen to chat and observe. Her meat and potatoes resembled my mother's hearty cooking. It was the delicately seasoned salads and the way she cooked fresh vegetables that I found a welcome change. Peace and orderliness reigned in this female household. I loved being there with the three of them.

After our meal was over, Kim suggested I spend the night and catch my old bus to school in the morning. I readily agreed. Later in the afternoon, I walked down the street to see the house I once lived in. It felt odd to find another family there. Butch Sheel, my good friend, neighbor, and classmate, now had my paper route.

To be ready for school the next day, Jill and Martie went to bed at nine. After prayers and good night kisses, Kimberly turned out the lights in the bedroom they shared and closed the door. At the time, I was brushing my teeth and washing my face. When I came out of the bathroom and turned toward the den, I was surprised to see Kimberly in lounging pajamas ensconced on the bed, reading a book. As I entered the room, she looked up at me and said, "Johnny, why don't you get into your pajamas and come read a while?"

Obediently, I went back to the bathroom, changed my clothes, and followed her lead in reclining against the headboard with my legs straight out in front. Lying there side-by-side with our bodies slightly touching, I felt a strange awkwardness and tingling sensation. Kimberly chatted for a minute or two about her book. We read for about a quarter-of-an-hour; talked some more; and went back to our reading.

More relaxed now and deeply engrossed in the history text I held above my lap, I didn't notice what was going on below. All of a sudden,

I sensed something moving through the fly of the briefs I wore under my pajama pants. Looking down I saw Kimberly's hands bringing my stiffening penis out in front of us.

Shocked at this sight and the sensation of her touching me in a way I'd never experienced before, I watched in silence as she stroked the shaft of my growing erection, and fondled my swollen crown. "Oh, Johnny," she said while caressing me, "it's as soft as velvet!" In the minute or so that followed, I sat there rigid and speechless, not knowing what to say or do. Pangs of remorse then overcame her. She slumped forward, buried her head in her hands, and began to cry. "Johnny," she sobbed, "I've ruined a beautiful friendship."

Slowly coming to my senses, I put my arm around her and embraced her for the very first time. I held her tight, almost feeling pity, and told her not to worry, that I was all right. During the couple of minutes she rested in my arms, my head swirled with unfamiliar thoughts and emotions. Feeling reassured, Kimberly looked up at me with swollen eyes, and in a hoarse voice, said, "When you're married, Johnny, you can touch a person anywhere and it doesn't make a difference." These words seemed odd to me, and I thought to myself, "Yes, Kimberly, but we're not married!" By then, we were both emotionally drained and ready to part. I said nothing as she kissed me good night and went to bed in the room with her daughters.

The next morning, when I came down for breakfast, the girls were still asleep. As I approached the kitchen where Kimberly was at work, she stepped out into the dining room, looked at me sheepishly, and said, "I'm sorry for what happened last night. I was wrong to have done that."

"Don't worry," I responded. "I'm okay." It was getting late, so I ate quickly, grabbed my books and things, bid her goodbye, and dashed off to catch the school bus before it left at seven-fifteen.

On the bus to school that morning, as during the previous night, I could think only of the surreal events in the back bedroom, of being touched by Kimberly with her longing look and caressing hand, of her sobbing while I held her in my arms, and of her strange comment about being married. These images filled my mind and wouldn't let go. Throughout the day, as I went from class to class, I felt as if I was in a trance. Mr. Irwin, my history teacher and onetime baseball and basketball coach who knew me well, immediately noticed something was wrong. I was always one of the best prepared and most active participants in his class. That day, however, I was miles away as I stared blankly at the wall. He called on me a time or two during our class discussion, but I had to answer, "I'm sorry, Mr. Irwin, I didn't hear the question." I don't know what my other teachers thought of me, but soon enough I'd hear from Mother of Mr. Irwin's concern.

My sleep Monday night was as disturbed as it had been the night before. I tossed and turned, incessantly reviewing in my mind once unimaginable images and questions about Kimberly. During class on Tuesday, it was more of the same. Basketball practice was a chore. My body made the motions while Sunday night's scenario ran through my brain.

By Wednesday afternoon, I began to regain my energy and concentration on the court. That evening, the shock of our undreamed of encounter was finally starting to wear off. Lying in bed at night, my innocence so unexpectedly shattered, I struggled to make sense of it all. How could the woman I'd placed on a pedestal and hoped would soon marry her minister make such a move? Was Kimberly as attracted to me as I was to her? What were her intentions?

Whatever I concluded, consciously or not, the deep desire I had for someone to hold and to love ultimately determined my behavior, as it did Kimberly's. That she was my mother's best friend and twice my age made no impression on me. I was young, loyal, and love-struck. What the future might bring was the last thing on my mind.

Improbable Love

Mother, me, and Grandma Schultz, June 1959.

# Part II — *Experience*

## 9  Weekend Lover

When I arrived home from basketball practice late Thursday afternoon and was searching for something to eat in the kitchen, Mother pulled up at the side of the house with a car full of groceries, and honked. "Mom's home and needs help!" I shouted to my brothers, but they were too preoccupied to respond, so I went out alone to lug in the bags. As I approached the car, Mother greeted me in her usual airy way.

"Hello, sweetheart," she said. "How was school today?"

"Fine," I replied.

"I bumped into Mort Irwin at the shopping center this afternoon," she continued. "He told me he was concerned about you, that you had a far off look in class on Monday that made him wonder if something had happened to you. Is everything all right, John?"

"Don't worry, Mom, everything's okay," I said, then unloaded the groceries as quickly as possible, and began to think about dinner.

The following day, Kimberly called to talk with Mother. She wanted to know how everyone was, particularly me. Since Mother had quit her job at St. Clement's at the time of our move, she and Kimberly saw much less of each other, but talked a lot on the phone. Mother told Kim what Mr. Irwin had said. Kim was alarmed and asked that I call her after school. She also said she needed a sitter for Saturday night and wondered if I could come then.

Feeling more composed and self-assured, I called Kimberly right after dinner.

"Johnny, are you all right?" she asked. "Peggy's told me what your history teacher said—that you seemed inattentive and distant in class on Monday. I'm concerned about you, Johnny!"

"Don't worry. I'm okay," I replied.

Then she continued, "Maurice wants to take me out tomorrow

66

evening to make up for last week. Would you be willing to sit for the girls again?"

"Yes, I'll come," I answered, and we settled on six-thirty as the time she'd pick me up.

When Mr. Hopson brought Kimberly home at ten Saturday night, Jill and Martie were sound asleep. I studied at the dining room table while Kimberly was out, but had packed up my books and was just finishing up in the bathroom as she appeared at the top of the stairs. Kim greeted me in hushed tones and went into the big bedroom to change. Lying on the bed in my pajamas with my back against the headboard, I watched her pass by to use the bathroom. Then she came into the den.

As if an apparition, Kimberly stretched out silently beside me in the dimly lit room. No longer pulled up into a bun, her long brown hair cascaded down her back the way it did at the Mountain Place. The long fingers of her favored left hand found those of my right as our motionless bodies touched. My heart was beating so loudly I thought it would wake up the girls. For a couple of minutes, we sat there, looking straight ahead.

Suddenly shifting to face me, Kimberly said, "Johnny, I was foolish to say what I did last week."

"What are you referring to?" I asked.

"I mean, what I said about it making no difference where married people touch each other. Obviously, not all places are the same," she explained. "To touch a person in special places has special meaning. And, of course, I know we're not married. I'm sorry I said that."

"I'm not," I whispered after a short pause. As my arm wound around her shoulder, I pulled her to my chest and the anguish in her face melted away. Kimberly looked into my eyes, then closed hers, and offered me her lips. In our first passionate kiss, I moved my lips over hers till I found the right fit, and pressed hard. A few seconds later, she pulled back and said with a smile, "Johnny, I loved that kiss, but you're biting my lip." We both laughed, and I relaxed. This time I kissed her with more finesse.

After our long embrace, Kimberly started to reach through my fly to continue what she'd done the previous week. Changing her mind, she stopped, and pulled off both pairs of my pants. I was better prepared now, and sat there contentedly while she fondled and stroked. "Johnny," she said once again, "it's as soft as velvet!"

Kimberly was the first to touch me that way. I'd never done it myself and was not yet sensitized enough to give up my semen to her caressing hand. Wet dreams had always accomplished what she hoped to do. When Kimberly realized I wasn't able to come, she gave up and leaned back against the headboard.

Now it was my turn to explore. As I reached into her bra, she stiffened and hesitated to let me go further.

"I'm sorry I'm not well endowed in the chest, Johnny," she said shyly.

"That makes no difference to me," I replied as I touched her breast. Pushing for more, I unbuttoned her pajama top and she slipped out of it. Opening her bra was another matter. I tugged and pulled, but got nowhere until she maneuvered to remove it. Still uncomfortable about being seen, Kim cupped her hands over her breasts, but I persisted, and finally got my first glimpse of them. I felt their softness, and was touching her nipples when she said, "Go ahead and suck them, Johnny."

The smooth, clear skin of her arms, shoulders, and breasts made me eager for more, so I pulled off her pants. As she turned on her stomach, I ran my hand along the curves of her back and buttocks. From there, I went slowly down her thighs and calves to her feet. I had often admired her firm bottom and shapely long limbs. Now I was amazed to find myself caressing them.

Having surveyed Kimberly's naked body from the back, I gently rolled her over. Looking up, she pulled me to her, resting my head against her thumping heart. While in this embrace, I slid my hand down over her tummy to the hair and lips that guarded my goal. Feeling without seeing wasn't enough, so I moved on down beside them.

After I had explored here and there, Kimberly said to me, "Johnny, stick your finger in my hole."

I followed her instructions, but didn't want to stop at that, and said, "Kim, I want to come in."

Caught off guard, she paused a few seconds, and responded, "Johnny, I'm not prepared for intercourse right now. I don't have my diaphragm in, and besides, once one starts down this road, it's impossible to stop. Now's not the time. It's too early for this."

We kissed and held each other tight once again, but were emotionally spent. I was also ill at ease, suffering pain and congestion from the lack of an orgasm. Though she offered to try once more, I felt it was time to quit, so we put on our night clothes and parted with a kiss.

Sunday morning was bright and beautiful. Kimberly was up early, a holdover from her days as a Navy wife, and a sign of her energy and enthusiasm for life. When I came down, she was in the kitchen making pancakes. Beaming at me, she put her spatula down, stepped into the dining room to look around, then opened her arms and gave me a hug and kiss. The nature of our relationship was changing fast. I was elated, but strove hard to fathom it.

Before they went off to church, Kimberly suggested I join her in attending a service at St. Clement's. My dream of having someone to hold and to love seemed to be coming true. Through Kimberly, the emptiness I'd long felt on Sunday mornings could also be filled. Later that day, together with Jill and Martie, she drove me home.

Mother was happy to see them, and insisted they come in. As soon as he heard Kimberly's voice, Charlie hurried down from his bedroom and sat beside her, as if to say, "Look, big brother, you're not the only one she likes!"

If Kimberly hadn't already given up the romantic designs she had on the pastor of St. Clement's when she broke the barrier between us, she did so immediately thereafter. From then on, she was happy to consider Mr. Hopson a "dear friend," whom she would see in church on Sunday, and whenever he asked her out to dinner.

I would continue to babysit for her girls when needed on the weekend, but also began to stay with the three of them even when there was no need for a sitter. My record was such that Kimberly and I had the perfect pretext for my visits. After a while, however, any pretense of babysitting fell by the wayside, and it was enough for me to say to my family that I was "going to stay at Kim's."

The next step in our rapidly evolving relationship came the weekend following our second intimate encounter. On Saturday afternoon, I rode to Fairlington with my mother, who came in to say hello to Kim and her girls before going off to Grandma's house. After Mother left, I took my things, including a suit for church, up to the closet in the den. When I came down to see what was new, Jill and Martie were baking cookies while Kimberly supervised. Once the cookies were done, we gathered at the dining room table to devour them with milk. Then I strolled over to say hello to my grandmother.

Following dinner and a chat with Kimberly, I sat down in the living room to read until it was time for some favorite TV shows, which the four of us watched in the front bedroom. Jill and Martie had twin beds that were pushed together between the two front windows. Kimberly's bed was near the bedroom door. When the programs were over, it was time for all of us to turn in. I said good night and went to bed in the den.

Lying on my side facing the open door, I wondered what would happen next. A time or two, I heard someone in the other room cough, toss and turn; after a while, everything went still. Some minutes later, there was a soft rustling sound in the big bedroom, followed by faint footsteps moving through the dark. As my heart pounded faster, I looked up to see Kimberly coming to me in a long, gossamery gown, a moment I'd been waiting for all week.

"I've missed you, Johnny," she whispered, sliding in beside me.

"I've missed you, too, Kim," I replied, as I smelled her sweetly scented body, and enveloped her in my arms.

Although somewhat more accustomed than before, I still had a hard time believing we were together this way. Stroking her legs thrilled me, the way it did the previous week, but once I reached her freshly trimmed mound of Venus, I soon left them behind. Halfway through my upward journey, her tummy made a soft resting place for my face, then I continued on to her nipples and to her waiting lips. Thanks to my teacher, I was learning life's lessons quickly.

Gazing into Kimberly's eyes, I was eager to open a new chapter in our relationship.

"Kim, I want to come in," I said. "I want to be with you."

"Johnny, I don't think we're ready for this yet," she responded. "Nothing's more powerful than sexual intercourse. Once you start, there's no turning back." I clearly heard what she said, but my desire for her was overwhelming and I kept pushing hard to reach my goal.

"I don't have my diaphragm in," she continued. "It's old and hasn't been used in years. I'm not sure it'll hold tightly over my cervix."

I felt a bit sheepish about my ignorance, but asked anyhow, "What's your cervix, Kim?"

Seeing my lack of knowledge called for further instruction, Kimberly said firmly, "Johnny, you've got to know how a female's built if you want to be a good lover. Go quietly and get the flashlight on the desk over there, and come here and look!"

When I returned, Kimberly parted her legs for a firsthand view few new anatomy students got. I peered and poked around, then touched a swollen pinkish place that made her start and shudder. That, she said, was her clitoris. For good measure, I rubbed it again.

Upon completion of this lesson, Kimberly got up and disappeared into the bathroom. I'd never seen a sight like that. I had, however, seen a diaphragm, but didn't know what it was. While helping my mother with housework several years earlier, she gave me her apron to wear. For some reason, I reached into its pocket, where I found a thin, round, rubber cap with a thick but flexible rim. I held it up to examine it, then put it back again. Mother said nothing as I did this, and neither did I, but I remember thinking that was what I used to see sitting on a dresser in my parents' bedroom while we played there.

After a minute or two, Kimberly returned to the den, snuggled up to me, and reached down to check on "Little Pricky." To her, everything was "little this," "little that," or "little so-and-so," no matter how large the object or person might be. In this case, Little Pricky was as big as he'd ever get. She helped me out of my pajama pants as I hoisted up the skirt of her nightgown, then she gently pulled me on to her and into the intimacy I longed for.

Lying motionless in a tight embrace, we gained a new sense of each other. Our heights and builds were very compatible. As we would soon discover, so were our ages sexually. That night, however, my plumbing still wasn't working. After pausing a while, we tried again, but I couldn't come. Kimberly told me she was "feeling a bit raw inside," and I was starting to ache, so we parted for the night.

The congestion I felt the previous week was nothing compared to what it was now. In place of testes, I had two lead balls. I moved this way and that trying to relieve the pain, but nothing I did was to any avail, so in desperation, I got up and went into the big bedroom. Kimberly heard me approach and turned to find me beside her bed.

"Kim," I whispered, "this congestion's killing me." Saying nothing, she pulled me toward her and reached in through my fly. As I leaned over her, she gave me a firm rubbing that led to relief. At the moment of coming, my whole body tensed, I gave a start, and shook with a new kind of pleasure, which brought a satisfied smile to Kimberly's face. It had taken several tries in a couple of weeks, but the logjam was broken and my ability to function now established.

Sunday morning, I went to St. Clement's with Kimberly and the girls. Their mother and I accompanied them to their Sunday school classes, then I followed Kim into the windowless sanctuary, where a large cross hung timelessly above a granite altar. Ten years had passed since I first peeked into this modernistic temple and watched the parishioners enter and leave from my vantage point across the street. Sitting there with Kimberly at my side, I could further see how fast my life was changing. The blare of the organ broke the calm that enveloped us and Reverend Hopson appeared in his resplendent robes to start the service. I was not a singer, nor was I familiar with the liturgy, so all I could do for the next hour was sit and watch what Kimberly and the others did. Before taking communion, she whispered, "Johnny, you'll have to stay here while I go up to the altar. Only those who are confirmed can partake of the consecrated bread and wine."

When the service was over, I followed Kimberly to the door, where our preacher was greeting the congregation. Mr. Hopson welcomed me warmly. "How nice to see you here, Johnny," he said. "I hope you'll join us often." During teatime that followed in the parish hall, Kimberly introduced me to the friendly parishioners as "Peggy's son, Johnny, who babysits for the girls." Kimberly's companionship, warmth, and affection transported me. Going to church with her helped satisfy another of my needs.

On the Saturday after Thanksgiving, Kimberly surprised me with another turkey dinner. An even bigger surprise awaited me that night.

As I lay in bed, waiting and wondering what would happen next, she came to me and said, "Johnny, the girls are asleep now. Let's go down to the living room, where we won't be so close to them." Kim loved Jill and Martie dearly, and didn't want our deepening relationship to harm them in any way.

To create a nocturnal bed, Kimberly placed a sheet and pillow on the carpeted floor next to the piano. Wide open radiators and our ardor for one another kept us warm. The shock and disbelief I felt at Kimberly's first advances were now largely gone, and I was eager to take up where we'd left off the previous week. To suck at her breasts, I pulled down the top of her nightgown, then peered into appreciative eyes, which she closed when I kissed her. After caressing her from head to toe, I went to the magical place and joined my body with hers. Embracing each other tightly in the soft light coming through windowpanes at the top of the front door, we flowed to and fro like undulating waves until we achieved simultaneous release.

Our passion temporarily spent, Kim opened her eyes widely and exclaimed, "Johnny, *I went over a mountain!*" I hadn't heard this expression before, but experienced the same ecstasy she did, and felt proud of my power to satisfy my lover. A couple of times that night, Kimberly told me, "You're so gentle with me, Johnny." I didn't know what her previous experience had been, but was pleased she was grateful for how I instinctively treated her. From then on, our lovemaking was as fulfilling as it could be. It also proved Grandma Schultz was wrong—men don't have *all* the fun.

When I awoke in the den the next morning, Kimberly was standing beside my bed fully dressed. I looked up to see her radiant face and hear her say, "My dear, you've overslept. It's time to get up for breakfast if you're going to church with us." Sitting and standing beside her in the sanctuary and the parish hall that morning, I was even more in love, if that was possible.

## 10 Only *Sixteen!*

My turn of fate was remarkable. In three weeks I'd gone from a sexually inexperienced and socially unengaged schoolboy to the weekend lover of a sophisticated woman only four years younger than my mother. Most of my classmates, if they fell in love at all, could hardly have dreamed of what I was doing.

As my relationship with Kimberly progressed, my thoughts turned to her even more than before. The sound of her voice thrilled me. So did her name. I didn't have to say "darling" or "my love"—"Kimberly" said it all. I thought of her constantly—while riding the bus to and from school, in the halls between classes, and especially at night as I lay in bed listening to music on the radio before falling asleep. What I waited to hear most of all was Johnny Mathis' quintessential love song, "The Twelfth of Never." I was transported by its haunting melody and lyrics, which I addressed in my mind to Kimberly, particularly the words:

> *You asked how long I'll love you, I'll tell you true,*
> *until the Twelfth of Never, I'll still be loving you.*

For the first time since developing a longing for someone to love and to hold, I felt fulfilled.

We talked on the phone several times during the week, usually after she and Mother had conversed. Sometimes, Kim would ask for me directly. Often, however, Mother took the initiative. "Johnny," she'd say, "Kimberly's on the phone. Would you like to talk to her?" I knew from personal experience my mother's thinking could be more wishful than rational, but her feminine intuition was nearly infallible. She readily discerned when someone was in love, especially one of her sons. Being the romantic and matchmaker she was, she did whatever she could to facilitate our relationship. Frequently driving me to Fairlington also gave her the opportunity to see Kimberly as well as her mother.

With the passage of time, my sexual prowess increased, as did my desire. Lying in bed listening to the sounds in the next room while Kimberly waited there for her daughters to fall asleep, my teeth would clatter and my whole body would shiver and shake in anticipation of our pending rendezvous. Time passed slowly, as if an eternity, and I could hardly stand the pressure building up inside me. Finally, after some coughs, shifting about, or calls in the dark, everything quieted down. I then heard the welcome sound of a swishing gown as Kimberly descended the stairs, signaling to me the coast was clear for love.

Our first time together was the speediest. Afterward, lying side by side, we'd embrace, kiss, and commune. Before too long, I was ready to make love again. The third time was a slower affair, often with Kimberly on top. When it was over, sometimes at one-thirty in the morning, both Kimberly and I, our passion spent, would be off to bed with a hug and kiss. On occasion, just before going upstairs, she'd let her tongue hang out to show contented exhaustion, and we laughed at our own intemperateness.

Academically, my junior year of high school was demanding and crucial to college admission. Rising early during the week to go to school, with lots of homework to keep me up late, basketball practice and games, meant there were times after such trysts that I was too tired to get out of bed for breakfast or church. Kimberly, however, never seemed to be fatigued and went about her morning chores the way she always did. Still half-asleep and feeling as if I had a hangover, I'd see the sun shining into the darkened room around the pulled-down window shade and kick myself for still lying there, the slave of my gonads, instead of being up and out in the world. Later in the morning, dressed in her Sunday best, Kimberly would come into the room to check on me. Despite my fatigue, I could still get aroused with her at the side of the bed. Sensing this, she'd reach in under the covers and rub me to climax with an amused expression on her face. Even more exhausted than before, I was ready for celibacy until we were together again the following week.

To wake myself up on such occasions, I stood under the shower with the hot water beating down on my head. During my oblivion to the world, Kimberly sometimes peeked in at my youthful body. How did I know? She told me so.

For the first few months, we were lucky with our lovemaking. Shortly after I arrived one Saturday afternoon, things seemed to have changed, and Kimberly appeared upset.

"Johnny, my love," she said, "we've got a problem."

"What's wrong" I asked.

"I've got the curse," she explained.

"What's that?" I responded.

"I've got my period. We can't be together tonight," she told me.

"Why not?" I wanted to know.

"I thought you might find it disgusting," she answered. "Some men are turned off by the sight of a menstruating woman."

I had seen bloody sanitary pads before—never a woman bleeding that way—but the thought of not being with Kimberly for this or any other reason was far worse than any messiness that might occur.

Once she saw this prospect didn't bother me, she voiced another concern. "Johnny, you should also be aware that a woman can get pregnant during her period, but the odds are against it. In any case, we must always be careful."

Kimberly was as observant and curious as she was sensitive and caring. Beauty in general, and the male body and sex in particular, attracted her attention. She once told me of the surprise she got as a girl when, walking along the side of a swimming pool, she looked down at a man who was lying there sunning himself. With her trademark smile, a mixture of amusement and amazement, she said, "I saw this thing sticking out from under his trunks."

"What did you think?" I asked.

"Oh, I was fascinated," she continued. "I kept walking by him until one time I got too close and almost stepped on him. He got irritated and told me to watch where I was going!"

I seldom had reason to quarrel with Kimberly. On one occasion, however, I did become upset with her and told her so. This occurred one night as I lay upstairs on the bed in the den and heard her tell an old colleague of her husband's who had taken her out to dinner, how my mother once tried to masturbate in the shower. After the friend left, she came to tell me the coast was clear.

"Kim, when someone confides something in you, you shouldn't betray that trust!" I admonished her.

Although somewhat taken aback, she replied, "Johnny, you're right. I'm sorry I did that."

To hear intimate secrets about one's parents creates a strange feeling, especially in someone still young. I'd seen and done a lot by then, so I was not shocked the way many teenagers might have been. Sooner or later, we all learn that parents are people with problems and desires as much as anyone else, though sometimes we'd be happy not to know.

On one occasion, when we went down to the laundry room in the common basement to do a load of wash, Kimberly recalled an incident with an older neighbor of hers whom I had recently met. This man, a retired military officer, pleaded with Kimberly to have sex with him. His wife, he said, had been sewn up because of cervical cancer, and he was suffering terribly from deprivation. He knew Kimberly was a young Navy widow and hoped she might take pity on him.

"How did you answer him?" I asked.

"Oh, I felt sorry for him," she replied, "but, I told him no."

A couple of times, after we made love and were engaged in intimate conversation, Kim got a wondrous look on her face and exclaimed, "Johnny, that's amazing!" She was referring, naturally, to "Little Pricky." "When he's asleep" she would say, "he's a little guy. But when he's awake, how *big* he gets!" I wasn't thrilled about his being a little guy, but was happy he could rise to the occasion to astound and satisfy my experienced lover.

In turn, there were things that surprised me. Kimberly would sometimes mention that a man she'd seen was built in such and such a way, or that he bulged this way or that. I soon found out she wasn't referring to the muscles of his arms or legs.

Kimberly also talked about marital problems a friend of hers was having with her husband, the assisant pastor to Mr. Hopson. He was, her friend complained, "too big" and hurt her when he penetrated her.

One afternoon when we were alone in her living room, Kimberly stood close to me, looked up and said, "Johnny, I love you!" I hadn't heard these words from her before. They were crucial to me and to our relationship. When I replied, "Kim, I love you, too!" I said the obvious. I had bonded to her the way a duckling does to its mother.

The affection we had for each other and the time we were spending together told my mother that something serious was going on between us. Some mothers pump their sons to learn about their activities or feelings; my mother did not. Like most teenage boys, I never told her anything about my sexual life. All the same, she intuitively knew how madly in love I was. Perhaps, too, when she did the laundry or emptied the trash, she wondered what had happened to the traces of wet dreams she no doubt had seen before. Or perhaps she thought I'd discovered masturbation. But there were no signs of that, either.

Mother liked to talk with Kimberly about me. When she did, Kimberly didn't try to hoodwink my mother or hide her affection for me. In fact, my mother once told me Kim said she would marry me if I were older. In turn, I heard from Kimberly of Mother's remark that I was probably the manliest of her sons, to which Kimberly agreed. If Mother was trying to learn about our relationship, this kind of probing didn't get her very far.

Finally, Mother came right out and asked, "Kim, are you and Johnny sleeping together?"

To this question, Kimberly replied, "Why Peggy, Johnny's only *sixteen!*"

That seemed to satisfy my mother, or throw her off balance. Most likely, her suspicions never ended, but her inquiries did.

Following Kimberly's recounting of this conversation, she looked at me in wonder, breathed deeply, and confessed, "After I said that to Peggy, I gulped."

Mother's interest in knowing about us didn't stem from fear that Kimberly might mistreat me or do me harm. She had too much faith in Kimberly as a kind and caring person to think that. Nor would it have occurred to her that such a relationship could damage me developmentally. She knew I was responsible and mature for my age, and saw how I blossomed in the company of a person we both loved. A romantic to the core, Mother was in love with the idea of love and affairs of the heart. What she missed in her relationship with my father, she sought in stories of romance and the lives of people she knew. The possibility that her son and her intimate friend were lovingly engaged in a sexual relationship and truly enjoying each other's companionship would have given her much vicarious pleasure. It was my mother, after all, who made the match between us in the first place.

Not long after Mother's query, Kimberly looked me directly in the eye and spoke with a seriousness I'd not witnessed before.

"Johnny," she said, "I want you to promise you'll never tell Peggy about us."

"I won't," I told her. That was a promise I made willingly, and kept for fifty years.

Kimberly needed me as I needed her. We were compatible and happy together. Mother often remarked what a handsome couple we made. In fact, we seemed to have everything going for us but age. This significant difference soon caused me much distress and pain.

## 11 Trying to Catch Up

Not too long into our new relationship, when we entered the sanctuary of St. Clement's together on Sunday morning, or chatted with people during teatime in the parish hall, I began to feel self-conscious standing next to the self-assured woman I adored. I was sixteen; she was thirty-four. In bed and in our affection for each other, we were equal partners. But in the eyes of the world, she was a mature adult with children and I was still a boy. For family, friends, neighbors, and strangers, we needed an explanation, so I was always "Johnny, Peggy's son, who babysits for the girls."

I loved Kimberly, and she loved me, but we couldn't show it. We had to be careful whenever we walked together that we didn't hold hands. We had to watch our words, so we didn't say "I love you" in front of her girls. We had to beware of how we touched or looked at each other in order not to give our secret away. Late at night, when we used the bathroom after making love, Kimberly remembered not to flush the toilet twice for fear her neighbor, Niela, would hear this through the common wall. Kim was also mindful that our voices didn't carry through as well. Whatever the circumstances, we had to pretend we were other than the lovers we were.

Eighteen years had passed since Kimberly was my age. She was married, then widowed, and had two daughters who were only six and seven-and-a-half years my junior. She had done more in life than I, had more language, and knew more of the world, such as books, foods, people and places. She experienced things I hadn't even thought of. I learned much from this teacher of mine, but I longed to be her full partner, not just her pupil. I never thought to myself, "If only she, too, could be sixteen!" Instead, I would have given eighteen years of my life to be thirty-four.

Kimberly was my woman and I wanted to be her man, which

was more than I could fully be. I suffered from something no amount of love, effort, or book learning could make up for—youth, inexperience, and a lack of financial means. In time, I came to understand that some of life's lessons come only with living and age. At sixteen, I didn't have the requisite amount of either to cope with feelings of inadequacy and jealousy. Despite our unequal situations in life, Kimberly treated me with respect and understanding, never with condescension. When she took down her hair to make love, these differences between us disappeared.

As time went on, I learned more about Kimberly and her past. I saw the inner strength and toughness that had gotten her through the long struggle with cancer that took her husband's life. Her mother, who had the same name, died of cancer not long before. The Kimberly I knew was a devoted mother. No doubt, she had been the same as a wife. Her faith in God and her church was firm, but not overbearing or proselytizing. I'm sure she didn't see our relationship as contradicting her commitment to either her children or her religion. She was energetic and physically strong, someone not easily scared. When the piano had to be lifted off the floor in order to pull a rug out from under it, she did the lifting, she told me laughingly, while Mr. Hopson did the pulling. A shrewd judge of character, her mind was sharp. She liked to jest, was quick to laugh, and enjoyed a joke. Kimberly could be frank when it was called for, but by nature was diplomatic. I liked her levelheadedness, efficiency, and neatness. She was sincere and compassionate, and understood life's ironies. Above all, her *joie de vivre* and sparkle made her company a pleasure. She lifted my spirits and made me soar.

The shapely legs and derrière I loved to see and touch were due in part to dance training. She took ballet for years as a girl growing up in northern New York state, where her father taught geology and anthropology at a university, and also served as curator in the university's museum. When her father retired, he worked a few more years for a local company. Kimberly recalled that when she was young, her father, who had an M.S. and an unfinished Ph.D., went back to school at Harvard, but found it difficult to continue and gave it up. Her older sister, Jill, was the student of the family. Jill went to college at one of the Seven Sisters, got married to a stockbroker, and settled in Massachusetts, where she had several children. On my trips with Kimberly, I came to meet all her relatives, including the lady whom her father married after her mother's death.

Kimberly could have gone to the same college as Jill, but instead chose a finishing school in the Washington, D.C., area. Its two-year curriculum emphasized both academics and social graces that prepared young women to act intelligently and properly once out in the world. She wanted to marry her high school sweetheart when he graduated from the Naval Academy two years before she would have finished a bachelor's degree. Over Christmas break of her second year, the U.S. Army, in fighting the war, took over the school, so she missed out on her last semester. Whatever the reason, Kimberly never achieved the kind of intellectual self-confidence she should have had. "Little me," she'd say to me in a tiny, self-deprecating voice whenever she felt inadequate or challenged academically. This bothered me, because I thought it was unwarranted. Both of us were students despite our age difference and supported each other's efforts.

In June 1943, following his graduation and commission in the Navy, Kimberly and Bruce Blake were married in Annapolis in the Naval Academy chapel. A sonar expert, Bruce went to sea to track enemy submarines. Kimberly once admitted to my brother, Dick, that she and Bruce did too much drinking while he was stationed in Key West. Following the war, Jill was born, then Martie.

For three years, Bruce suffered from a rare cancer of the eye. When first discovered, he and the family were still in Florida. How the disease came about, no one knew for certain, though some pointed to sonar radiation. The first signs appeared one day when three-year-old Martie accidentally elbowed her father in the eye. Experiencing great pain, he had to see a doctor. For two years, things went on without resolution until, in 1953, the family moved into their Fairlington home so Bruce could go to the Naval Hospital in Bethesda, Maryland for treatment. During this final year, his condition progressively worsened. The cancer spread throughout his head and disfigured his face. Kimberly told me that while this was going on, a violent rainstorm flooded their basement. All the things they had stored there—most importantly, family mementos and pictures—got soaked and largely ruined. Bruce was despondent and wondered aloud if God was trying to obliterate all traces of him. Finally, he succumbed and was buried in Arlington Cemetery. Other than memories of her high school sweetheart and dashing young husband, his death left Kimberly at thirty-one with the tightly folded American flag that had draped his coffin, two young daughters, and a small government pension.

Making love to Kimberly came naturally, but being comfortable with who I was did not. Feelings of jealousy and despondency sometimes enveloped me like a dark, heavy cloud. These moods could be set off by the sight of Bruce's picture on Kimberly's desk, or a casual comment about him or them. He was the father of her children who died only a few years earlier, and was still part of her frame of reference, not a distant or fading figure. These reminders of him threatened me. Was Kimberly comparing the two of us? Who was better with her in bed? Did she love me as much as she loved him? Kimberly was my first love and everything to me. I wanted to possess her totally, the way she did me. But I was not her first, which tormented me.

Despite my jealousy, Bruce's untimely death affected me deeply. I wept in my heart for him, a young man robbed of life far too early, for Kimberly, a young wife without a husband, and for Jill and Martie, children who lacked a father. At times, this knowledge made me feel guilty, as if I were an interloper, someone who was unrightfully taking his place. But I also knew I could never be or do that, because I was always running behind, unable to catch up in age and experience to do what he could have done. Yet, Kimberly and I were lovers and my passion for her consumed me.

I was sensitive about the way I appeared to the world, as well as how Kim referred to me or us. When an old male friend or a couple came by to pick Kimberly up and take her out, my youth stared me in the face. She introduced me as "Johnny, her good friend, Peggy's, son, who came to babysit." It didn't mattered that Kimberly and I were lovers, that as soon as her guests had left, we'd be lying together on the very spot where they were standing. When they brought Kimberly home and sat down with her in the living room to chat, I'd hear them talk about places I'd never seen or couldn't even locate on a map. I wasn't able to compete with people twice my age who had done exciting things before I was born. What did I have to offer Kimberly other than my body and companionship?

Sometimes, when she came home from an outing, I smelled alcohol on her breath and became upset. Was it because, like the Southern Baptists I knew in Sunday school, I thought drinking was sinful? Or, was it because I, who had never had an alcoholic drink in my life, knew that drinking was something only adults could do legally?

I was a boy who desperately wanted to become a man overnight, but did childish things that belied my wish. Unexpectedly, one afternoon, Niela from next door popped in to visit while I was at Kimberly's. Self-conscious about my presence there, I hid in the basement until she left. When Kim came down to tell me Niela had gone, she said, "Johnny, you didn't have to hide!" I had no money but pocket change, whereas Kimberly ran a household and was raising two children closer to me in age than I to her. Financially, I was a burden on her with my large appetite. How could she not see me as a child as well? Our radically different circumstances gnawed at me.

On rare occasions, something happened that led Kim to use mildly sharp words with me. Such incidents almost made me sick to my stomach. "Kimberly, take me home," I'd say, but she quickly remembered who I was, and acted to smooth things over. Once in a while, however, when Kimberly got into a snit, I would tell her, "Kim, you're not at your best!" and that would calm her down.

When I fell into a melancholic spell, I withdrew into myself, retreated to the den, and listened to music on the radio, my mind befuddled and incapable of coping with the thoughts and feelings that overwhelmed me. Occasionally, even after making love, I would stand in the kitchen until three in the morning listening to music on the radio. When Kimberly realized I wasn't upstairs, she would come down after me and plead with me to come up to bed. Trying to soothe my pain, she enveloped me in her arms, patted my back, and said, "there, there," the way she comforted her daughters when they were hurt or in distress. Then she would urge me to try to express my emotions rather than keeping them bottled up inside me.

To allay my fears and jealousy, Kimberly advised me, "Johnny, I want you to know a person's heart can grow bigger and bigger. Bruce was my husband for eleven years and will always be a part of me. But there's room in my heart for more than one, and I love you, too."

When I was overcome by despondency about catching up to her, she tried to reassure me by saying, "Johnny, my dear, you're just at the beginning of your life!" or "You have a whole lifetime to look forward to!" Sometimes, too, I heard, "Johnny, I don't want you to worry. One day you'll have a beautiful young wife and family, and will forget all about me." That, however, wasn't what I wanted her to say. "Kim," I'd reply, "you're the only one I ever want."

With Kimberly's help and the passage of time, I got better at dealing with my feelings of despair and began to express them. Sitting on the bed facing her with tears in my eyes one sunny afternoon, I took a small step in this direction. "Kim," I blurted out, "there's an image in my mind that haunts me."

"What's that, Johnny, tell me!" she exclaimed.

"It's of me running hard after a train I can never catch," I said, hardly able to utter the words.

The mirror I saw myself in when I was with Kimberly and her peers didn't reflect the same way when she looked at me. At thirty-four, signs that distressed her were starting to appear. She noticed laugh lines in her face and would point them out to me, as she did barely visible spider lines around her eyes. These or any slight blemishes she thought unbecoming she covered with makeup or powder. Seeing the passage of time in me and my contemporaries led her to declare, "Johnny, how perfect you are! There's not a line or wrinkle on your face!" At other times she remarked, "With all those beautiful young girls with flawless faces at school, why do you even bother to look at me?"

Once in a while, she alluded to the slight bulge in her tummy. Varicose veins in her calves and thighs embarrassed her to the point that she had a doctor take them out. None of this alarmed or bothered me. She was charming, beautiful, and caring—a friend with whom I could speak and be heard, and who talked openly and sincerely with me in turn. What more could a person wish for? Yet, ringing in my ears were things I really didn't want to hear.

## 12  My Woman

During the Christmas break, I spent as much time as I could at Kimberly's house. When she began to worry about what others might think, I repaired to my grandmother's home for a while. From there, I hitched a ride to basketball practice with a teammate who lived nearby or borrowed Grandma's or Kimberly's car.

Grandma Schultz was always happy to have someone to talk to, especially about what was happening with her next-door neighbors and friends, their adopted children, and their endless family problems. She never pried into my affairs. Even if she had, she probably wouldn't have minded what I was doing, because it was her expectation that "a man has all the fun."

In a comment dated 1/30/58 on the back of my second quarter report card for U.S. History, Mr. Irwin wrote:

*I'm extremely glad to see John beginning to unbend a little bit. There are many other things in life equally as important (and sometimes more so) than the highest academic achievements.*

Mr. Irwin was a personable man. In his coaching and teaching, he did me many favors over the years. His comment was, I believed, an indication that my relationship with Kimberly was having a beneficial effect on me. The love I had for her and received in turn helped me feel better about myself in general and more self-assured. My bouts of melancholy were slowly abating.

The varsity basketball team I played on my junior year was a strong one. Among our tallest and top players were Garland Schweickhardt

Basketball teammates Scotty Strother (lower left), Jim Simpson (upper left), Gar Schweikhardt (upper right), and me, winter 1958.

and David Lockman. The best ball handler and shooter was Ronnie Terwilliger. Six-foot-three Jerry Gerich, a high jumper who seemed to have springs in his legs, was the junior who played the most. I saw action as a substitute in a forward position, and Scotty was a substitute guard.

With our cheerleaders on the court, and Kimberly and her girls sometimes rooting in the stands, we were winning left and right. After the game was over, the three of them would wait for me outside the locker room. As I came out, I could hear Kimberly say, "Over here, Johnny," then see her wave, and watch her face light up. This attention didn't escape my teammates, or Mr. Robinson, the varsity coach, from whom I had to get permission to drive them home. On the bus back to school one time, I heard from a friend, one of our co-captains was peeved at the special treatment I received, and confronted the coach. "How come Wertime gets to ride home separately, and we don't?" he wanted to know, a question Mr. Robinson squelched with a curt "Shut up!"

Each time I went home with the Blakes, Scotty would come up to me the next day at school and say with a laughter-studded grin, "I didn't see you on the bus after the game. What's going on with you and that woman of yours?" We'd chortle together, and I'd remind him she was my mother's best friend and I merely babysat for her daughters. Such protestations, however, never quashed his suspicions or inquisitiveness.

In gym class the first two grading periods of eleventh grade, I got A's from Coach, my former basketball mentor and one-time neighbor, but in the third, I ended up with an unheard-of C. In his remarks on the back of my report card, Coach cited me for fifteen absences from class, a lack of interest in wrestling and gymnastics, and poor effort. I don't recall what the absences were about, but wrestling and gymnastics weren't my favorite sports, and I showed it. If I wasn't good at something, I usually didn't want to try it.

My performance in Coach's class and what he probably saw of Kimberly and me after games and in Fairlington must have weighed on his mind. How much it did I learned one afternoon late in February. As I was walking down the court at the end of our final scrimmage before the start of the Northern Virginia High School Basketball Tournament, I saw Coach standing alone off to the side. He beckoned to me and I went over to him.

"John," he said in his deep, quiet voice, after greeting me with a nod, "I've seen you and your sugar mama together a number of times recently. Be careful of her. She can hurt an innocent fellow like you."

This stunned me and I asked, "What's a sugar mama, Coach?"

"A woman who keeps young men as playthings," is what he told me. Hearing these shocking words, I looked at him in disbelief.

"I'm sorry, Coach, you don't understand!" I exclaimed.

"What don't I understand?" he asked.

I hesitated a moment, then confided in him, "If you promise to keep it a secret, I'll tell you the truth. She's not a sugar mama. We *love* each other!"

From the startled look on Coach's face, I could see my well-intentioned advisor was as unprepared for my rejoinder as I was for his warning. Following the few seconds it took for my reply to sink in, he looked me in the eye and responded, "Don't worry. I won't say anything. You've got one on me."

"What's that, Coach?" I asked, then blurted out, "Do you

mean…?"

By now, Coach was walking towards the gym door, and answered back, "If you don't know, then never mind."

My naiveté blown away, I thought to myself, "Yes, Coach, you're right. I do have one on you."

In my love-struck state at the time, I gave little thought to Coach's warning and my newfound insight, and never mentioned this incident to anyone, not even to Kimberly.

Wakefield handily won the the regional tournament and a berth in the state finals in Charlottesville, the first time a team from our young school would play in such an event. To fire us up and send us on our way, Mr. Irwin arranged a pep rally in the gym for the entire student body, with cheers for each of us on the eleven-man squad.

In our coats and ties, we traveled in several cars to the old field house of the University of Virginia, where our accommodations turned out to be bunk beds in the middle of a large open dormitory for visiting teams. Mr. Robinson had settled on this arrangement because of a lack of funds. Since none of us had ever been in such a place or situation before, we had few expectations, and made the best of our quarters. Soon after settling in, we went out to practice. Our first game was the next day.

That night in the field house was a fiasco for the team. The old bunk beds weren't comfortable, we had no privacy, and were worn out from the excitement of being there. To top it off, some of our teammates became rambunctious and noisy, while strangers came and went until early in the morning.

Charlottesville was a beautiful, small university town in 1958. The opportunity to play basketball in a state tournament was a great experience for us. For me, as great, if not greater, was the pleasure of seeing the quadrangle designed by Thomas Jefferson and being in the charged atmosphere of a famous university. Having homework to do, and caught up in the spirit of the place, to the surprise of my coach and the ribbing of some of my teammates, I headed off to study in between our Friday morning practice and late afternoon game.

After hunting around a while, I finally found a niche for myself in the law school library. Appropriately dressed in a coat and tie like the others in the paneled reading room, I felt good appearing to be more than a high school junior. The experience also helped to put me in a mood for thinking about college, as I'd be applying in less than a year.

In the semi-finals, we lost to a lesser team by only a basket. Wakefield was cold and lethargic, unable to get going until the end. This was a wake-up call to Coach Robinson, who contacted our school to demand funds to lodge us in a motel. That night, Scotty and I shared a room, and along with the rest of the team, got a good sleep, which helped the next day in the rout of our opponent for third place. After showering and dressing, my teammates and I huddled together to watch the championship match, which we all knew we could have won had we been better rested the previous day.

Before I left for Charlottesville, Kimberly told me she would be there Saturday to watch the final round and take me home. I had counted on this since the previous weekend, when the Northern Virginia tournament and homework preempted our time together. I was an addict; if I missed a weekend with her, I nearly went into a frenzy.

When I finally located Kimberly, I was all set to take off. Much to my surprise, she told me my parents, who had never come to one of my basketball games before, were there with her, and that Dick was home with the girls. I realized my plans had been dashed and struggled to contain my disappointment.

"Jesus, Kim," I said, "why did you bring them along? Couldn't they have driven down on their own? I thought we were going to be together tonight. And, Dick's there to boot!"

"Johnny, I couldn't help it," Kimberly responded. "They wanted to see you play and I couldn't say no to them. Your brother's with Jill and Martie because I couldn't find anyone else who'd stay late. I'm sorry!"

Like my father, I was unable to hide my emotions well. As I drove Kimberly's car in anger up Route 29 at seventy-five miles an hour with one hand on the wheel, Kimberly and my parents sat there in silence, too petrified to say a word.

Along the way, I pulled off to get a soda at a roadside store. Kimberly got out of the car at the same time I did, hoping to calm me down. As we were going in, she was starting to say, "Now Johnny," as she always did when she wanted to advise me about something, but suddenly stopped when we came upon a teammate standing in a narrow aisle. Kimberly had seen him from the stands and while milling around after games, but never face-to-face like that. I was caught off-guard by his presence, but recovered and made an introduction, which created a strange feeling in me. It hadn't occurred to me I would ever have to introduce my lover to one of my peers, so removed from each other's worlds they seemed to be.

This brief encounter helped break the bad mood I was in, and made the rest of the trip home less tense. Back in Arlington, my separation from Kimberly didn't last long, for the next evening, Mother dropped me off at her house after we attended one of our confirmation classes at St. Clement's.

Other than being Protestant, I hadn't been sure what I was, but I knew what I wasn't—Roman Catholic. Before the days of ecumenical goodwill that Pope John XXIII initiated in the Second Vatican Council opened in 1962, there was a hard edge to Protestant-Catholic relations that I felt growing up in Fairlington. Many of my pickup football games and organized baseball games were with boys who went to parochial school, particularly Blessed Sacrament. Snide remarks or points of religious doctrine meant to needle or challenge a Protestant were frequently interspersed in our banter. These could hurt, especially when delivered with certitude that truth was on their side and a Protestant's fate was eternal damnation—points I wasn't equipped to dispute scholastically. Fairlington neighbor and baseball teammate Billy Veeder, who wielded his quick mind and sharp tongue to better effect than his bat or fielding glove, was particularly memorable as a young warrior for the Catholic faith.

The antipathy our Catholic peers showed Protestants was mild compared to what they had for non-Christians. The worst epithet in the arsenal of the five Irish Catholic Kirwin brothers, who lived in a nearby community called Parkfairfax, was, "You Jew!" I heard this repeated so many times growing up that it created a reluctance in me to use the word Jew in referring to anyone of that faith, a sensitivity assuaged by saying "Jewish" instead. The nuns who taught my Catholic teammates prepared them well for doctrinal battle, but did little, it seemed, to mitigate a deeply ingrained bigotry.

To obtain confirment in the Episcopal Church, my mother and I needed to fulfill two requirements—attend eight catechism classes Reverend Hopson taught on successive Sunday evenings, and demonstrate knowledge of the Church's teachings and practices at the end. If they had been rigorously observed, Mother wouldn't have been confirmed, for she didn't get to every class, and hadn't been able to learn all the requisite material. Concerned, she confessed to our minister that her preparation was incomplete. Knowing my mother well, Mr. Hopson, in his inimitable way, said, "Peggy, don't worry about it. Your heart is pure. It's your intentions that count in God's eyes." The relief these words brought Mother was palpable. To have failed confirmation class would have been a devastating blow to the former church secretary.

On March 30, during a Sunday morning ceremony in the sanctuary of St. Clement's, Bishop Goodwin confirmed my mother and me, and a number of others, as members of the Episcopal Church. Kimberly watched this happen and beamed as I took my seat beside the two most important women in my life.

Kimberly fed me well when I was with her and her girls, satisfied me sexually and socially, and gave me guidance in growing up. Her support and encouragement now helped me establish a connection I had long sought. Was that the work of a sugar mama?

One Monday morning following a confirmation class, I woke up at Kimberly's feeling sick to my stomach.

"Kim, I don't feel well enough to go to school," I said.

"Johnny, you have to," she replied. "What will Peggy think I've done to you if you don't go?"

Seeing how sensitive Kimberly was this way, I got dressed and went off to catch the bus. Before noon, I ended up in the clinic with a fever and upset stomach. Mother came and took me home. I was in bed for a day or two, long enough to demonstrate I wasn't trying to play hooky.

## 13  Night Alone

In April, Kimberly and I celebrated two birthdays, my seventeenth and her thirty-fifth. We also celebrated our first night alone. During the week-long spring break, Jill and Martie attended a three-day church program in southern Virginia. Kimberly and I dropped them off, then drove home, stopping on the way for a bite to eat. Arriving at Kimberly's just before dark, we stretched out on her bed to rest from the driving we'd done.

Before long, we were petting and becoming aroused. Kimberly went into the bathroom to prepare for lovemaking, but came out exclaiming, "Johnny, my diaphragm's got a hole in it!" I jumped up to see what she was talking about. Holding it up to the light, Kimberly said, "We can't make love tonight using this! The risk's too great. I could easily get pregnant. You'll have to go buy some condoms, or we'll have to forget about it." I'd been spoiled by my lover in the previous months, and hadn't taken any precautions of my own. In truth, I'd never used a condom before, nor had I even bought one.

"Go to the drug store and get some condoms if you want to make love" she repeated.

"Where should I go?" I asked. "If I go to Bradlee, someone might see me buying these and wonder what I'm doing. Besides, what kind should I buy?"

"You can take the car and go to Shirlington," Kimberly declared. "It's less likely you'll bump into anyone you know there. If you don't get a good quality, like Natural Lamb, you won't feel much. Go on, now, before it gets too late! The drug store closes at nine."

I had no inhibitions whatsoever with Kimberly, but did have buying a pack of condoms. After surveying the only drug store in Shirlington, I found the shelf with the contraceptives. When I was certain no one was looking at me, I got close enough to read the labels. Becoming familiar with the various brands and prices took more time.

Suddenly, someone came my way, so I moved off to another part of the store until the coast was clear. Then I returned to my quest with a renewed sense of purpose, because it was getting late and I wanted to be with Kimberly on our first night alone. Seeing they were out of the brand she'd mentioned, I was standing there wondering what to do next, when the store lights flashed on and off a time or two, and a clerk cried out, "We're about to close!" Now desperate, I asked the clerk manning the door where I could find a pharmacy still open. "You can try the one in Green Valley" he said.

Although not far away, this all-black community was a place I'd never visited and knew only by its reputation as an unfriendly neighborhood for whites. "Which will win out," I asked myself, "unfounded fears or my desire for Kim?" It didn't take long to reach a decision. Soon I was pulling up in front of the well-lit Green Valley Pharmacy. I walked in slowly and looked around. The pharmacist saw I was young, white, and nervous.

"What are you looking for? Perhaps I can help you find it," he said.

Trying to appear as nonchalant as possible, but turning a bit red in the face, I answered in a dry, raspy voice, "Natural Lambs." Before I knew it, he had a package of three on the counter.

"Is this enough?" he asked.

"Yes it is. Thank you very much," I replied.

Just after I paid him and had taken a few steps toward the door, I heard a voice from behind me. "Hello, my friend," someone said. "I haven't seen you in quite a while!"

I stopped dead in my tracks. I'd been spotted, but didn't know by whom. When I turned around, standing there smiling was my old pal, Bill, the black janitor at Fairlington School.

Bill was an affable man in his late thirties, someone I visited frequently in the school boiler room when classes were over for the day. In summertime, with little to keep me busy, I went by to see him as often as I could. We got along very well. Even after I left elementary school, I kept in touch, but with our move to north Arlington, our contact had lapsed.

Talking with Bill again was like old times, so pleasant, in fact, that I nearly forgot my mission and the embarrassing bag in my hand. Suddenly, I realized how late it was. Apologizing for my rush, I told him I had to get home on some urgent business. After I left, the pharmacist and he must have had a good laugh.

When I got back to Kimberly's house, I went upstairs and found her asleep. I undressed, lay down beside her, and held her tight. A minute later, she opened her eyes, looked at me, and said, "Johnny, you've been gone a while. Did you have any luck?"

I showed her what I'd found. She looked pleased and told me to open one of the condoms. As I was doing this, she cautioned, "Be careful you don't tear it."

Before I slipped it on, I told her, "Kim, I want you to take your nightgown off. I don't want anything between us tonight."

To wake up in the morning beside my naked lover was an exciting new experience, one I wanted to have all the time, as married people do. To me, Kimberly was like my wife, if only fate would have let her be.

After experiencing love in the morning, we took our first shower together. Peeking in wasn't necessary that day. Another new sensation— the feel of her wet skin against mine—came as we hugged and caressed under the cascading water.

## 14  Baseball

Following the end of basketball season, the boys' gym at Wakefield became the site of indoor baseball practice. Soon after returning from Charlottesville, a number of us were back on the wooden court readjusting our eyes and reflexes to a much smaller, harder ball. As soon as the weather warmed up enough, we went outside, usually in early March when it could still be quite cold and windy. That was my least favorite time of year, when the ball would sting my hand whenever it hit my bat or glove. A true hot weather sport, baseball never felt right until late in May or early June.

Of my teammates, the one I knew best besides Scotty was Garland Schweickhardt, a catcher like me. During the summer between my sophomore and junior years, Gar and I played American Legion baseball together. Our coach, Lefty Freisem, put me behind the plate and Gar in the outfield. The highlight of the season for me was a line drive home run I hit, one my father witnessed and applauded. After the game was over, someone brought me a piece of wooden latticework the home run ball had broken through as it cleared the high left field wall more than three hundred feet away.

Later the same summer, Gar picked me up in Fairlington so we could play together in a basketball league in northwest Washington. He owned a car, and drove very well, but also very fast. Tearing through the narrow streets of Georgetown, Gar would get so close to the cars parked on my side I was sure the mirror there would get knocked off, or I would lose an arm if it strayed even slightly out the window.

During Gar's last high school baseball season, and as it turned out, mine as well, Mr. Irwin played him at catcher and kept me as a backup. I didn't resent this because Gar was a good catcher, a friend, and my ride home. The day games we played at Wakefield were on the diamond next to school. Even today I laugh out loud, as teammates and I did then, at "Come on Bobby, you're better than he *are!*" the girlfriend of an opposing team's pitcher shouted from the stands.

When our games were over, we returned to the locker room to put our gear away and shower before going home. On one of these days, our team co-captain, a short fellow named Lance, who ironically played first base, confronted me as I was leaving the shower room. With a scornful look on his face, he pointed at Little Pricky and remarked about his size. None of my peers had ever done that before. A year earlier, Lance's contempt might have taken its toll. Now, thanks to my relationship with Kimberly, which Lance probably had heard rumors about, I had complete confidence in what Little Pricky could become and do. Turning the tables on my teammate, I said, "It works well and I get to use it. What about you?" As I looked down at his face, I watched Lance's disdain turn to chagrin. After that, he never spoke a spiteful word to me again.

To warm up before our games, Gar pitched batting practice and I caught, which made me last to bat. He would lob them in and sometimes I belted the ball out of the park. Once, I hit seven balls in a row over the left field wall at the Four Mile Run field. By the third time I did this, most of the players on the opposing team came off the bench to watch.

Following a night game there in the middle of May, when we were packed up and ready to go home about ten forty-five, Gar said to me with a sly grin, "Wertime, I'm going up to Fairlington for a short while. Would you like to come along?" Why he thought I might have business there at that time of night I didn't know, but was happy to accept his offer. As we entered South Fairlington, my teammate asked, "Where shall I drop you off?" I directed him to the parking lot off to the side of Kimberly's house. "I'll be back in forty-five minutes" he said. "If you want a ride home, be right here waiting." I agreed to Gar's terms, and slipped out of the car into the still of the night. The air was balmy and sweet, and I was in love.

I knocked on Kimberly's door just hard enough to wake her up, but not her girls. She would get up fast, I hoped, for there was just enough time for a quickie.

It didn't take long before I heard Kimberly whispering, "Who's there?"

"It's Johnny," I whispered back.

"Johnny!" she said in surprise and delight as she saw me standing there. I was wearing my baseball uniform, which she'd not seen before. After looking me over with an approving smile, she opened her arms for a fervid embrace.

"Kim, we don't have much time," I warned. "My friend's going to pick me up in forty-five minutes. I can't be late!"

"I hope he didn't see you come in here," she said apprehensively.

"No," I responded. "I was careful to get out in the parking lot. We've got to hurry, though, 'cause time's running out!"

Kimberly hurried upstairs to the bathroom, while I, trembling in anticipation, undressed down below. Soon she returned carrying the sheet and pillow for our nocturnal bed. Our union that night was brief, but one I remember as among the best.

As I ran to the appointed spot, Gar pulled up right on time. With my shirt tail hanging out and my shoes and socks in my hands, I hopped in and he took off. We sat quietly all the way home, scarcely saying a word. Both of us were tired from a long day at school and our late night baseball game, but very contented with our activities in Fairlington.

One of the last games of the season took place on a school day afternoon at George Mason High in Falls Church. Having absentmindedly left my uniform at Kimberly's house following a game the previous week, I rode the school bus to Fairlington in order to get it. From there, I was hoping she would drive me back to Wakefield in time to go with the team. I got into my uniform well enough, but couldn't keep my hands off of my lover. "Johnny," she laughed and said, "you're going to be late if we don't leave now!" No matter how hard I tried, I couldn't let her go. Finally, we saw there was no use in even trying to make the bus, so she told me, "Take the car and go! As soon as the game's over, come back and the girls and I'll drive you home."

When I arrived at the George Mason field, I saw that my teammates had warmed up and were listening to the coach give a pep talk. As I approached, Mr. Irwin smiled at me and made a crack that caused everyone to laugh. Then he said, "John, I had you scheduled to start as catcher today, but think it would be better if you rested on the bench. You look as if you're all tuckered out." I was, and that's where I stayed.

During the last game of the season, I did catch, but my desire to spend time with Kimberly was eclipsing my interest in baseball. Furthermore, the fastballs I'd caught since I was twelve had so bruised my hand that I could hardly stand the impact any longer.

The next time I was at Kimberly's, she was uptight in a way I hadn't seen before.

"What's wrong, Kim?" I asked. "Is something the matter?"

"Johnny," she said, "I'm a bit worried. I haven't gotten my period yet."

"How late are you?" I asked.

"Two days," she replied. "It should come soon, but I could also be pregnant."

Up to that point, I'd never thought about this possibility. Kimberly was always careful to use her diaphragm, and the chances of her becoming pregnant seemed remote to me. But now, for the first time, the question arose, what would we do if she did become pregnant?

Kimberly gazed at me and said, "Johnny, I've thought about this a lot. I'd love any child of yours I might carry, but given the circumstances of our lives, I think I'd take the girls and move away some place where no one knows us, have our baby, then put it up for adoption."

Although I was trying hard to leave my childhood behind, I couldn't visualize myself as a father. This prospect alarmed me, but Kimberly's professed love for a baby of mine was deeply touching. Other than going to be with her for its birth and holding it in my arms, there was nothing I could see myself capable of doing. "Let's hope it doesn't happen" was all I could say. Her period came soon after that, so we never had to face such a heartrending situation.

At the sports banquet for varsity athletes at the end of the school year,

I won letters for both basketball and baseball. The large green "W" trimmed with white the coaches gave out was a big deal for my high school peers. Most who received one sewed it to the pocket of a white wool cardigan and proudly wore it in school, or bestowed its use on a girlfriend to show they were going steady. Having no intention of wearing it myself and no girlfriend to offer it to, I gave it to Kimberly and her girls.

## 15  Construction Job

The summer after my junior year, I worked for John Corembus, the builder responsible for our house as well as most others on our street and ones under construction nearby. A second generation Greek-American, in his brusqueness and reserve, he appeared to me much more American than Greek. "Unk"—his uncle from the old country—a small, deeply tanned man with shoulder-length curly white hair and a habit of humming American pop tunes, assisted him after a fashion. Although Mr. Corembus offered me an hourly wage of $3.75 in the spring, my first paycheck was calculated at $3.25. I didn't know if this was some kind of Old World trick or because Mr. Corembus thought my contributions weren't worth more than that. In any case, I said nothing to him or to Unk. I did, however, grumble about it to my parents and Kimberly. Mother and Kimberly urged me to talk with Mr. Corembus, but I thought it best to let the matter ride, fearing he wasn't too impressed by what I was doing. Whatever money I made, I tried to save for college.

At the start of my first day on the job, even before I could turn around to look his way, I knew who was addressing me when I heard, "Boy, get over here and pick up them scraps on the ground before I give you a boot in the ass!" The West Virginia twang and intonation of Fred Rowland were unmistakable, as was his choice of words. Fred was smiling when I saw his face. He always smiled when he gave me orders or uttered vile oaths. "Get going," he said. "We don't want no lazy college boys 'round here!"

Fred was a hard and fast worker, a man with swift intelligence his drawl and manner of speech could easily veil. He liked to chatter while working, as did his colleague, Jim. Most of the remarks they directed my way were about "poontang" or "woolybooger." They'd ask me if I'd "gotten any" last night, to which I could honestly have answered "yes" on some occasions, but chose to remain silent. Or they'd engage in bathroom humor. Fred would let go with a loud fart, then turn in glee and say, "Boy, you shit!" as if I had done it. Once in a while, he talked about the "A-rabs" and recalled his time in North Africa during World War II. Jim was a heavy drinker, and periodically disappeared for long periods of time. Fred was more levelheaded and rarely, if ever, missed a day of work.

After I was on the job a while, a tall, twenty-year-old black man called "Smitty" appeared. He was strong and efficient, but unlike the carpenters, quiet and dignified. Smitty lived near Leesburg, which meant he had a forty-five minute drive to work. He was the only one there at all close to me in age. When we hit a slow spell or when I returned after lunch, Smitty and I would talk, often about his interest in cars. I respected him and enjoyed his company.

In the early weeks with Corembus, I came home after work and collapsed, exhausted from the heavy labor, sun, heat, and humidity. Over time, I got toughened up and had more energy to do things in the evening.

Before showering, I stripped down to my pants and lifted weights in back of the house near the cellar steps. The first time Kimberly saw me doing this was around four one Friday afternoon when she came to pick me up.

"Gosh, Johnny," Kimberly said with a smile as she walked up our short driveway. "Didn't you work hard enough today?"

I was pressing with all my might and starting to groan, then exhaled and dropped the barbell.

"I want to get stronger," I replied panting, "and build up my muscles."

Although I strived to look more manly, she seemed satisfied with the way I was. While I showered and changed, Kimberly went into the kitchen to visit with my mother and to say hello to my brothers, as she normally did. Charlie was always happy to see her, and snuggled up for a hug.

On weekday evenings after dinner, my father and I often played doubles with two men who would meet us at a nearby tennis court. If we didn't get up a game with them, we'd play singles or take a walk. Dick and Steve frequently joined us as well. Despite the things we did together, Dad and I were never close. I participated as much out of a sense of duty as desire, yet I often enjoyed myself. Dad taught and helped me in many ways, as he did others in and outside the Wertime family. I loved him and respected his mind, discipline, and drive, but hated how he exploited and treated our mother, and at times, my brothers and me. Unfortunately, there was little I could do about his self-centered behavior.

Conversations with my father were a one-way street; my role was to listen to him talk. Rarely did he want to know about me and how I felt or thought. But then, I couldn't tell him about Kimberly and me or begin to carry on about the matters that occupied his far-ranging mind. Grateful to be exposed to such an intellect, I was also glad I could escape from home and the feeling of being a retainer to a lord. Many a time when I was away, Dad complained to my brothers about my absence. However, he didn't lack for helping hands around the house or someone to play ball with, and said nothing to me directly.

I don't know what Dad thought I was doing at Kimberly's. He must have found Kimberly very attractive, but never talked about her, and, when in her company, acted uncharacteristically subdued. Perhaps her charm and elegant presence even intimidated him a bit. To make a move on Kimberly himself would have been out of the question in view of mother's and my closeness to her. If my father had known the true nature of our relationship, I'm certain he would have approved, for Dad had secrets of his own. This I know from what he once told me with pride when I was still fairly young, that he had "a woman in every port," female companions he visited while on government missions in the Far East.

From time to time, my parents mentioned the French custom of a trusted older woman initiating a youth into the mysteries of sex, implying, but not saying outright, they considered it a good idea. To have a relationship of this sort at my age would have been a feather in my cap, not one that would harm me, my father could only have thought.

Nearly eight months had passed since Kimberly seduced me and

104

changed my life. During this time, I had been on an emotional roller-coaster ride, reaching the pinnacle of pleasure, then plunging into the depths of melancholy and despair. Kimberly helped me work through these emotions, and her perseverance was beginning to pay off. I was learning to be more expressive of my feelings, and starting to accept that my place in her heart was firm, but not the whole of it, the way hers was in mine. As I gradually became less bothered by her memories of Bruce and pictures of him, she in turn mentioned him less often and eventually removed his image from the den. I was also gaining self-confidence when I was with her peers. My life with Kimberly, to use her words, was becoming more and more "on an even keel." Our great lovemaking continued, but doing things together and enjoying each other's company was as important to us.

That summer of 1958, Kim and I were becoming a couple, and with her daughters, a family, despite our unusual skew in age. I worked hard helping to build houses during the week, and looked forward to their company on the weekend. Kimberly picked me up Friday afternoon, or my mother gave me a ride. To be ready for work early Monday morning, I returned to north Arlington on Sunday evening.

One Saturday, we drove out through Front Royal to Skyline Drive to enjoy the beautiful vistas of the Shenandoah River Valley. After stopping along the way for a picnic lunch, we continued as far as Big Meadows, where there was a lodge and restaurant. Close by lay the meadows themselves, at dusk full of grazing deer. Up the road from the meadows, we found a hiking trail that went downhill along a creek. As we exercised our legs to break the journey, the girls exercised their tongues in complaint as they got more and more exhausted from the heat and humidity.

Kimberly was appropriately attired in Bermuda shorts, deck shoes, and a sleeveless blouse over a padded bra she didn't completely fill. Walking across some slippery rocks, I grabbed her upper arm to steady her. When I looked over to see how she was, I noticed I could see half way into her bra, which gave me the urge to do some exploring. While grasping her arm, I extended my middle finger as far as it would go, and found I could touch her nipple. This sly brashness caught Kimberly off guard. The first time I did it, she gave a little yelp and jump, then a lusty laugh. Every so often, I tickled her this way and she responded, but then she warned me, "Johnny, we've got to be careful the girls don't see us when you're doing this. I think you'd better stop."

When we got home that night, the four of us went to bed early. The long ride and exertion in hot weather had tired out the girls, who soon fell asleep. Taking her cue from this, Kimberly descended to our spot on the living room floor, and I quickly followed. Both of us were sunburned, so we had to be careful as we kissed and caressed. Just as I pulled the top of her gown from her shoulders, we heard footsteps in the bedroom and realized someone was starting down the steps.

"Mommy, where are you?" Jill was calling.

I leapt up and ran into the kitchen as Kimberly pulled up her gown.

"Jilliilee, I came down for a drink and am on my way up," I heard her say.

Kimberly met her half-asleep daughter at the foot of the stairs, close to where we were lying. Martie, a sounder sleeper, didn't make a peep.

I hid in the kitchen until things upstairs quieted down. Dressed again in my pajamas, I lay on the floor hoping Kimberly could return. What seemed like forever, but was probably half an hour, passed before that happened. We escaped our first close call without any damage, but now knew even better we had to be on guard to prevent harm to the girls and to our relationship.

## 16  Starlit Night

For the Fourth of July weekend, my mother wanted Kimberly and her daughters to be with us again at the Mountain Place. As before, I drove them up in their car. When we pulled in beside the Upper House, Mother was in the kitchen making lunch. "They're here!" someone shouted, and soon a small crowd came out to greet us. The Blakes were more comfortable this time, having already met nearly everyone there. Unlike the previous year, this visit was to be a sleepover.

With so many people to lodge that weekend, the question arose—where would our guests sleep? An aunt and uncle and their four children always occupied the old chicken coop the family converted into a bunk house across from the outside toilet. My parents shared the double bed in the front bedroom of the Upper House, while Dick, Steve, and I usually occupied the back bedroom. When Charlie was still a baby, he slept in the crib in the front bedroom with our parents, but now that he was six-and-a-half, things got more complicated. Sometimes he slept in the back bedroom on the double bed with one of us brothers, while Dick, Steve, or I went into the living room to a bed along the front wall next to the porch. Once in a while, Charlie slept out front. Clearly, there would be no place in the Upper House for the Blakes unless a number of us went up to the sweltering attic.

The solution I favored was the one my parents proposed—that Kimberly and her daughters sleep upstairs in the old log cabin with me there to look after them. The issue of lodging now decided, I drove Kimberly's station wagon down to the Lower House and unloaded it while Mother walked with them and helped them settled in.

Almost without fail, the Fourth of July holiday was among the hottest and most humid days of the year at our family retreat. That was the case in 1958. With the gear in place and the beds made up in the loft above the kitchen, everything was ready, I was hot and sweaty, and aching for a swim. The ladies changed into their swimsuits upstairs while I got into mine down below. Then, we went out to the pond.

Our small mountain stream fed the pond through an underground pipe from the side, as did springs welling up from underneath. The water was sweet, but very dark from leaves that settled on the bottom, making it hard to see more than a foot below the surface. In swimming across the pond, one went from warm to cold and warm again on the way from the small sandy beach to a long pier that jutted out into the water, something Dad had built. From there, we dove in and swam out to a float big enough to hold six adults or a greater number of children. An iron ring hanging at the end of a cable fastened high up in a tree along the back bank gave those not afraid the opportunity to swing out, drop into the water, and crawl back up to go again.

The only drawback of our pond was the algae bloom it got when there was little rain and the stream flow dropped. A green slime on the surface of the pond didn't bother most of us in the family, for when we swam around, it soon dissipated. However, it did leave a slick green film on the body. I liked to think of it as some kind of nutrient rich treatment, but not everyone was so forgiving.

Kimberly wasn't finicky, and went into the pond and out to the float. Less adventuresome, Jill and Martie stayed behind. After the sun had beaten down on their heads and backs for a while, and an enormous horsefly, which bit ferociously, buzzed around their ears, they started to change their minds. As they stood ankle-deep in the water, I thought I'd help them out. I picked Jill up and threw her in while Dick did the same with Martie. Finally wet and enjoying it, they paddled out to the float with us at their side. Kimberly, who was back on shore, was happy to see her daughters mingling with all the children. Along with my mother and Charlie—the family fish—she swam out to us.

Later that afternoon, my brothers, father, relatives, and I played badminton with our guests, who also tried their hand at pitching horseshoes. When her turn came, Kimberly stepped up to the peg, took aim, and with her strong left arm made a vigorous toss that went wild and hit Uncle Joe's big toe. Astonished by what she had done, she ran over to apologize. "I'm so sorry, Joe," she said. "I didn't know my little old arm could throw one of these so far." While apologizing to my uncle, Kimberly alternately squeezed and stroked his arm between his wrist and elbow. No harm was done to Uncle Joe's foot and, from his beaming face, it was clear he didn't mind this kind of apology, either. Seeing Kimberly do that, I was reminded of the menacing look she got when she once touched a stranger's arm this way. I pointed out to Kim the possible consequence this practice could cause her. She said I was right and told me she would stop doing it, but it never really ceased, so ingrained was her habit.

After our evening meal, Kimberly and I, together with my parents, sat around the living room of the Upper House chatting with the adults who remained as their children and my brothers played games with Jill and Martie. With the setting sun, Joe and Vee took off with their family, and the others went to the nearby bunk house. All that was left of the Wertime gathering that day were my parents, brothers, and I, together with Kimberly, Jill, and Martie. The girls were tired, so we said good night and headed down the narrow, winding lane toward the log house.

The sky that night was stellar. The moon and stars lit the way, while down below, fireflies put on their pyrotechnic show and the cicadas of the forest began a serenade. I walked in front looking carefully for any movement on the road or in the grass, for this was snake country. Once, we found a copperhead sleeping under the plank leading out to the diving pier. Another time, a copperhead and her two young ones were coiled and ready to strike down by the pond. A rattlesnake or two had also appeared by the Upper House, as did some harmless black snakes. I cautioned our guests about these serpents, but didn't want to frighten them into becoming like my mother, who was famous in the Wertime clan for her morbid fear of anything that slithered.

As we passed by the glimmering water of our now soft and sensual pond, I proposed a moonlit dip, but Jill and Martie had had enough for the day, so Kimberly got them ready for bed and I guided them to the outhouse. After she tucked them in, the two of us headed hand-in-hand for the pond.

Kimberly stopped to marvel at the incredible sky, but I kept on going, eager to plunge into the water. I swam to the float, where

I deposited my swimming suit out of sight in back. The freedom and exhilaration of swimming naked made me shout, "Kim! Come on in, the water's fantastic!" Hurrying up, she swam to my side and into my arms.

Treading water and kissing, I pulled down her suit and grabbed her breasts, causing her to laugh excitedly. The sensation of our bare bodies touching in the fresh mountain water gave us a thrill we couldn't contain.

Then, I whispered, "Kim, I want to come in."

She let out a loud, nervous giggle as my finger probed her crotch, but replied, very quietly, "Johnny, my love, I'd like nothing better, but we can't do it here. There's too great a risk."

The racket we made during our nocturnal frolic woke up Jill, who suddenly appeared to see what was going on. She sat at the end of the diving pier watching us as we cavorted in the dark water.

"Jill, come and join us," I cried. "The water's great!"

Kimberly backed me up with a motherly plea, "Go get your suit on and come on in, Jillilee. You won't regret it."

Jill wouldn't budge from her lookout, so after a while, I swam around to the other side of the float to put my swimming trunks on.

The next morning, as I walked up the lane toward the Upper House to check on breakfast, I met my aunt coming down to the water. Besides her swimsuit, she was wearing an enormous smile. "You and Kimberly seem to have had a good time in the pond last night," she said, the sparkle in her eyes as bright as the moon and stars had been.

## 17 Church Retreat

From the time I first met Kimberly, she talked a lot about a church retreat, where she was going to direct a summer camp. Later on, I heard her speak of the counselors who worked with her there and ministers she had met. Until she reminded me on the way home from the Mountain Place that she and the girls would soon be going there again for over six weeks, I hadn't thought much about this camp or how it would impact my life. Now, I did. Before they left, Kimberly told me she would contact me about coming to see them.

During the first three-and-a-half weeks of their absence, I wrote to her often. She wrote back to me, but in language that was guarded. I understood the reason for this, but craving her affection, I felt hurt, nonetheless. In one of her letters, she invited me to visit. After work on a Friday afternoon, I took the southbound train to a station where Kimberly was waiting to greet me.

As I entered the terminal, I saw her big smile and long, waving arms, and heard her call out "Johnny!" I was looking forward to a warm embrace, but the hug I got was as guarded as the letters she had written. One never knew who might be watching us there, she cautioned. Until we got to the privacy of her car, I almost felt like a stranger.

Sitting side-by-side, the distance between us began to recede. I looked at her with longing eyes and she did the same to me.

"Johnny, I've missed you," she said, words I readily repeated. On the way, she took my hand whenever she could, told me about the girls and her work at camp, and wanted to hear about me and my family. However, there was one thing she needed to tell me before we reached the retreat, "Please don't feel hurt if I don't spend all my time with you while you're here this weekend. The second session has just begun and these younger girls require a lot of attention. I'll be with you as much as I can."

Dinner was over when we arrived, but the lady who ran the kitchen had put some food aside. I was delighted to be there, sitting at a dining hall table across from the camp director, eating and talking away. After dinner, before we rounded up Jill and Martie for bed, Kimberly showed me around the beautiful grounds with their hundreds of trees—elegant elms, maples, and lindens—alongside natural growth sycamores and cedars. She also introduced me to some of the counselors, all of whom were older than me.

During summer camp, Kim, Jill, and Martie were the only ones who occupied a big house located at the highest point of the spacious retreat. I stayed there, too, but in a room on the second floor, at some remove from their own quarters on the first. Looking out my upstairs window, I could see the outdoor chapel, dining hall, swimming pool, and several other buildings.

That night, after the place was locked up tight and Jill and Martie were sound asleep, Kimberly came to me in my room. I was feeling lonely and isolated so far away from her, and hungry for her love. We hadn't been together for nearly four weeks. When she slipped into bed beside me, she was as ready for me as I was for her. In all the time we were lovers, I never had to beg or cajole her for the intimacy I craved.

Having Kimberly by my side in that unfamiliar house also reassured me, for at times, old childhood fears of the dark, the unexpected and unknown plagued me. These were set off by an incident that occurred at that camp the previous year.

Trusting in the Lord, the good neighborhood, and the relative seclusion of the retreat, camp policy didn't require the staff to sleep in the rooms with the young campers when Kimberly became director. All that changed one night when a man who appeared to be a counselor entered a dormitory and lay down in bed beside a girl. This person spoke very softly with her for some time, then began to position himself to rape her. Another camper, who was aware that something was amiss, got up as if to go to the bathroom, but instead ran to call Kimberly, who rushed into the room to find the stranger on the verge of penetration. Caught by surprise, the man scurried out on all fours, as if he were some kind of beast. The police came immediately, but the culprit had disappeared.

Kimberly said they suspected it was a local man with a detailed knowledge of the campus. Worked up by this memory, Kim then told me what she'd do if someone ever harmed one of her daughters. With the fierceness of a tigress on her face, she exclaimed, "I would claw out his eyes with my nails!"

The next morning, I saw Jill and Martie swimming in the pool and participating in various activities with the campers. They were growing up fast. From time to time, Kimberly mentioned how her older daughter "had sprouted tiny little rosebuds." Once in a while, when a blouse top flopped open, I couldn't help catching a glimpse of one myself.

Despite being a member of the Episcopal Church, I never felt at ease with displays of piety. Saying grace wasn't a custom we observed at home. The only blessing I was familiar with was what Kimberly said before dinner. It's good that I was, for as I waited with the campers and staff for the Saturday evening meal to begin, one of the retreat's administrators I'd met earlier in the day looked over at me and announced, "John Wertime will please say grace." A bit stunned at first, I thought to myself, "What'll I do?" Then the words I'd heard at Kimberly's, "For these and all His many blessings, may God's holy name be praised. Amen," came rolling off my tongue as if I had said them a thousand times. After dinner, Kim came up to me looking amused. "Well, Johnny," she declared, "you said that like an old pro!"

That Saturday night, I watched Kimberly leading the evening program for the girl campers. During an earlier session, Kim once told me with a big laugh, the girls were engaged in a discussion of "The Purple People Eaters," a highly popular song at the time. She joined in, but garbled the title by changing "people" to "peter," much to their merriment.

Among the people I met during this visit was the big and handsome fourteen-year-old son of a local minister whose name was also Johnny. Like the natives of the area, he had a pronounced accent I always enjoyed hearing. Kimberly told me with amusement how she was sitting behind him at a service in the outdoor chapel when his hand happened to stray and land on her closely shaven calf, which he stroked for a few minutes. When the service ended, he got up and walked away as if nothing had happened. This story made me pause a bit, and wonder what she might have felt for the other Johnny. My pangs of doubt and incipient jealousy didn't last long, however, because I knew Kimberly visited my bed, not his.

The church retreat I visited was a place of beauty, where Kimberly could be with people who were both congenial and dedicated to the beliefs she held. Her warm and gentle way, combined with her outgoing, laughing, good nature, meant she got along with everybody and was loved by all, campers and staff alike. I could never figure out why she wasn't nabbed by someone in the community there or among those she knew in the Episcopal Church. In any case, I considered it my good fortune to have her for myself.

All too soon, my two days were over, and I was on the train heading home. Kimberly, Jill, and Martie returned to Fairlington several weeks later.

## 18 Camping Trip

For some time, Kimberly had wanted to take her children on a camping trip to Cape Cod. While l was with them during my short visit to the church retreat, she asked me whether I'd go along.

"Of course," I replied.

"You'd better check with Peggy and Ted to make sure this is all right with them," she advised. On the way back from Cape Cod, Kimberly added, we could stop in New York state to visit her father and his new wife not far from where she grew up.

To accompany them meant quitting my construction job earlier than I had planned, which I didn't mind. We talked about sharing expenses, and agreed on a contribution from me of $75. This was no problem, either, since I had money saved up. When back home, I discussed the trip with my parents, who thought it was a great idea, but, Dad reminded me, I would "miss the family vacation at the Mountain Place." I didn't say it, but was very happy that would be the case.

For the trip, we needed a four-man tent, which we rented from a store in downtown Washington. The salesman showed us how to put it up. I wasn't particularly adept at feats of engineering, but got the general drift. Kimberly also bought sleeping bags for the three of them plus a big cooler. At home, I had my own sleeping bag and a Coleman stove from Boy Scout days.

The day after I left my job, Kimberly came over with Jill and Martie to pick me up. She thanked my parents for letting me come. I took leave of them so I could help the Blakes pack up and load the car for the start of our journey the next morning. As I was going out the door, Dick shouted, "Have a good trip, you lucky bum!"

In the car and ready to go by seven, we set out with Kim at the wheel.

She was to go as far as the New Jersey Turnpike, then I would take over. I'd had a license since I was fifteen, but had never before been in the driver's seat for as long as I would be with them.

Although it seemed we had to stop every hour and a half to use the toilet or get a snack, all in all, things went smoothly enough until New York City, where we hit heavy summer traffic on the other side of the George Washington Bridge. I crossed in the right lane, but suddenly discovered I needed to be in the left in order to follow the route the AAA laid out for us. Dreading the idea of making a wrong turn and getting lost in that madhouse, I slowed down and put my blinker on to shift lanes, but no one would give an inch no matter how frantically I signaled with my hand. The cars behind me were honking wildly and a traffic cop up ahead shouted, "Come on, Virginia, or I'll send you home in a box!" After many cars had ignored my plea, a compassionate soul finally appeared and let us cut in to get beyond the surly cop and on our way to the Cape.

We spent the first night of our family adventure in Connecticut. After driving around a campground for a few minutes, we settled on a site. Getting off the road and on my feet brought great relief. Kimberly and her girls were ready for it, too. The camp was filling up fast, and we already had neighbors on our left and right. I lifted the heavy tent out of the wagon and onto the ground. Kimberly gave me a hand erecting it, which went better than I had anticipated. As we were working, Jill and Martie hovered over us, wondering when we would eat. "Go look around and see what you can find," Kimberly told them. "Dinner will take a while. First, Johnny and I've got to get things arranged in the tent."

While the girls were off exploring, we had to figure out our sleeping arrangements. Jill, Martie and I had lived in close proximity for some time now, and were used to seeing each other in pajamas and swimming suits, but had never slept an arm's length from each other, as we would that night. Kimberly suggested we put her daughters next to one another on one side of her and me on the the other.

"That's fine with me," I said. "The only problem is, I've got to get up in the middle of the night to pee."

Kimberly knew this and replied, "I guess you'll just have to step over me when you have to go. We've got to be very careful of what we do together. I know it's not going to be easy lying so close this way, but we can't harm my girls." With that said, we finished arranging the interior of the tent, then went out to light the stove and begin preparing our meal.

Standing around waiting to see how I could help, I noticed a couple of men twice my age or more in conversation at a campsite next to ours. One of them saluted me with a can of beer, then called over to see if I'd like to join them. Not knowing what to do, I looked to Kimberly for guidance. At that point in my life, other than a sip of beer, a beverage I immediately disliked, I had never had an alcoholic drink, nor could I legally have had one. Kimberly gave a nod of encouragement, and followed up by saying, "Go have a good time! I'll be fine here alone."

I self-consciously went over to introduce myself to our neighboring campers, shook hands, but declined their offer of a beer. They talked a bit about themselves and their families, and asked where we were from and headed. I filled them in and chatted as maturely as I could as they eyed me up and down and Kim at a distance, no doubt wondering all the while about us and the girls. Kimberly and I must have appeared enough like a couple for one of them to pose a probing question in terms of "my wife." That was the first time anyone had ever referred to Kimberly this way. I, in fact, had come to feel she was indeed my wife, but had never used this term myself. Instead of answering, "Oh, she's not my wife, she and her kids are just good friends," I merely called her Kimberly in replying to the query, thus leaving them more perplexed than they were before I came over to visit. To avoid further scrutiny, I said something about having to help get dinner ready, and bid them goodbye.

When I returned to our campsite, Kimberly was dying to know how my visit had gone.

"Well, Johnny," she quipped with a grin, "at least you didn't run away immediately! What did they talk about?"

"Oh, nothing much," I said, "just about their families and travel plans. They also wondered about ours. One of them referred to you as my wife."

Hearing this, Kim's eyes lit up and her grin grew even broader,

117

then she clapped her hands and let out a loud laugh of amused delight. Soon thereafter, Jill and Martie returned red-faced and out of breath. They'd joined some kids their own age in playing ball, but now they were hungry and ready for a meal.

This incident reminded me of an experience I had shortly after I'd finished ninth grade. While Dad attended a conference at the University of Vermont in Burlington, we brothers looked around town with our mother and took our meals in the university cafeteria. I towered over them and no doubt appeared to shepherd them about. On our second morning there, while we were in line for breakfast, one of the cafeteria workers came up to Mother and said, "My colleague and I are having an argument, and I want to settle it once and for all." Pointing to me, she asked, "Is he your husband or your son?" My trim thirty-seven year old mother was both flattered and amused, while I stood there blushing. Little did I know then that I would find myself in a similar situation a couple of years later.

Our first night in the tent was a difficult one for me. With Kimberly lying so close in the dark, it was hard to keep my hands off her. However, fatigue eventually overcame temptation and at dawn I was still asleep beside her.

After breakfast, we headed for Cape Cod. Our goal was Nickerson State Park, near Brewster on Cape Cod Bay. All this was new to me and the girls, but not to their mother. At the entrance to the nineteen-hundred-acre woodland park, we got a map from the ranger and directions to our campsite, one of several hundred in the beautiful pine forest. As I drove along the winding road, Kimberly spotted our "own little place" situated toward the top of a slope that went down to the banks of one of eight kettle ponds, for which the park and Cape Cod are famous. These were formed over 10,000 years ago as glaciers retreated, leaving pools of crystal clear fresh water that fluctuated from season to season, depending on ground water and precipitation.

As I got out of the car, I heard the wind whistling through the trees. That mellifluous sound was with us the whole time we were there, and still plays in my ears. Our visit was also blessed by a clear blue sky, warm daytime temperatures, and cool nights. Unlike the campsite we had left in Connecticut, it was carpeted with pine needles and lay some distance from neighbors. If only my tent-erecting technique that day had matched the perfection of the weather and natural setting.

Everything went wrong from the moment I removed the tent from the car. No longer packed the way it was in the store, I had trouble handling it at first, then getting the support arms to stay in place. They kept falling down, sometimes whacking me on the head or back. Kimberly was there watching, ready to assist, but the sight of those bars and my flailing about made her laugh, and me increasingly irritated and impatient. At one point she suggested we ask a neighboring camper for help. Determined to do it myself, I'd have none of that. Much time and many softly uttered curses later, I got the tent up. By then everyone was hungry. As my companions prepared our dinner, I arranged the gear in the tent.

During our days on Cape Cod, we explored the park, walked around the ponds to gaze at their limpid waters, and watched people boat on a lake, fish, and play in the water. We thought of swimming, but one of the girls found the water too cold, so we kept on hiking.

We also visited nearby Brewster, a scenic town in the center of Cape Cod. From there, we drove to Provincetown at the top of the Bay, another pleasant place with lots of tourists, especially men. I could see Kimberly's amusement as she watched the handsome young bartenders making up drinks while dancing and jiggling about to the blaring pop tunes of the day, one of them a great song celebrating summer, with the refrain:

*It's summertime, summertime, sumsumsummertime.*

Then, as now, Provincetown was a famous gay vacation spot, something my strongly hetero brain only faintly took in.

The activities of the day and the coolness of the night made Jill and Martie sleep soundly, but didn't work any magic on me. Though the rational part of my brain commanded forbearance, my libido wouldn't cooperate with Kimberly lying next me. No matter how hard I struggled to control myself, I always came up short. I would touch her here and there, and she would turn away and face the girls or move down into her sleeping bag. Sometimes, too, she whispered stern warnings or made desperate pleas. By the third night, seeing the girls weren't likely to wake up, she reached over to me in the dark to find my sleeping bag unzipped and my manhood eagerly waiting. Always a resourceful person, Kimberly quipped, "There's more than one way to skin a cat." As her right hand held some Kleenex, it didn't take her strong left hand long to release me from my misery.

As soon as she did this, we both had to pee. We got up quietly and went out into the moonlight. There were toilets a short distance down the road, but it was chilly and we were too tired to bother. When we got far enough away from the tent and our picnic table, Kimberly instructed, as she hunkered down beside me, "Now Johnny, don't sound like a cow and wake up the girls!" For me, that wasn't a problem. At the Mountain Place, we boys used to relieve ourselves outside all the time. In fact, we even had contests to see who could pee the farthest. I knew how to spray this way and that to muffle the sound, but as a squatting female, Kimberly didn't have that option. While I stood erect, performing silently, she proceeded to be the bovine, the contents of her full bladder hitting the ground with such a racket our laughter might have awakened our neighbors. Fortunately, the girls slept through it all.

Kimberly used to say the colors blue and green shouldn't be worn together, that they made a "bilious combination." Maybe that was what they taught her in college, but to me, the sight of swaying green pines against a dark blue sky showed otherwise. I left that memorable park on Cape Cod only reluctantly.

From Nickerson, we headed west to Amherst, where Kimberly's sister, the first Jill in the family, lived with her husband and children. Kimberly introduced me as Johnny, her dear friend, Peggy's son, and told them how I helped her by babysitting and looking out for her and the girls. We stayed there one night, then continued on to northern New York state to visit Kimberly's father and stepmother.

Jill and Martie traveled well, but like all kids, when they got tired, they would ask, "When are we going to get there?" Most of the time, however, they sat in back and amused themselves by reading or drawing. Our inability to make love during this trip made it extra hard to keep hands off as we zipped along newly built highways. When my willpower weakened, I'd reach over to caress Kim's bare thighs and calves. Sometimes, I touched her erogenous zone and she reciprocated. During all this, we had to be careful we didn't speed up too much, or that little eyes weren't watching us, which happened one time.

The small farm Kimberly's father owned had a tiny guest house with two double-decker beds where the four of us slept. Arriving in the afternoon, we put our bags inside, then came out to visit. I didn't know how many times Jill and Martie had seen their grandfather, but it didn't seem to be a lot. His new wife was a most pleasant lady, who got along splendidly with Kim and the girls.

While Kimberly and I were outside talking with her father, I instinctively said, "yes, sir," or, "no, sir," in answer to his questions. He seemed irritated by this southern style of address, and told me to drop the "sir." Since I couldn't call him "Dad," and my habit was so ingrained I wasn't able to break it, I nearly reached the point of stammering in my conversation with him. It was clear to me Kim and her father weren't cut from the same cloth. Her personality, I thought, must have come from her mother.

At night, Jill and Martie occupied one bunk bed, and Kim and I the other. I took the bottom of ours so I could get to the bathroom without waking her up. When the lights were off and the kids were asleep, she whispered, "Good night, Johnny," and reached her long arm down to hold my hand. Instead, she got something hard and straight. Laughing out loud, she came down to help her young lover out.

We didn't stay on the farm for more than a couple of days before heading back to Virginia. Kimberly, the girls, and I had made the rounds, and I had met all of Kimberly's close relatives. Little did any of them know they had seen their newest would-be in-law. Despite the good time we'd had, it was a relief to be back in Fairlington, where our amorous life was more easily pursued. My other family was scheduled to be at the Mountain Place until the end of August, so I wasn't under any pressure from Dad.

In the newspapers we saw on arriving home was alarming news for those of us being educated in Virginia. The Federal Government

121

had ordered the Commonwealth to desegregate its public schools. In response, the powers in Richmond talked of shutting them down. Kim and I agreed that integration was morally right and resistance was wrong. But if both sides carried through, what would happen to us during the coming year?

We thought Episcopal High School might be a possibility for me. I could live with Kim or my Grandma Schultz in Fairlington and attend it as a day student. The trouble with this would be the considerable cost and the uncertainty I could get admitted on such short notice.

The issue became moot when the Federal Government decided a change of this magnitude should be phased in over a number of years, starting from the lowest grades. In time, the injustice of segregation came to an end, but this happened after my time with Kimberly and as a student in Arlington public schools.

## 19 Signet Ring

The time Kimberly, Jill, Martie, and I spent as a family in the late summer of 1958 marked a watershed in my relationship with my thirty-five-year-old lover. She and I had known each other for nearly two years, the first year on very different terms from the second. During the latter, I underwent a profound transformation. From a sexual innocent, I became an accomplished lover of a sophisticated woman. Our individual needs for intimacy and companionship coincided, as did our carnal desires. It's hard for me to think of a better sexual match than ours. The distance that separated us in worldly knowledge and experience, to say nothing of emotional maturity, was another matter.

My struggle with feelings of possessiveness and inadequacy, and the despondency I suffered, must have been as trying for Kimberly as they were for me. Her nurturing helped bring me a long way from where I started. Over time, I became better able to cope with my negative thoughts and to limit my melancholic spells. The even keel she kept was a comfort to me, as great as the pleasure I derived from her cheerfulness and enthusiasm for life.

By the beginning of my senior year of high school, we had achieved a closeness and regard for each other that committed couples have. The facade needed to protect our commuter-type relationship had become second nature to us. Virtually everyone in both of our families knew we were close friends and companions, but none knew the intimate details. In most respects, it seemed to me, we were made for each other, except for our ages. That fact molded the fundamental aspects of how we related, who took the initiative, made most decisions, and acted out of maturity. Above all, it determined who ultimately saw our destiny. Given enough time, I would gain the knowledge and experience I lacked, but not the years. We could overlook these discrepancies for a while, and did so with gusto until they caught up with us. In the meantime, the fact that I was just a teenager usually receded into the background when I was alone with Kim. What I most had to offer her was my love and companionship, virility, and unwavering loyalty.

To my surprise, one autumn day Kimberly had a present for me—a gold signet ring engraved with my initials, JTW. It was, Kimberly said, "A sign of her love and devotion." Taking what she said to heart, I put her ring on and wore it for years. When I went home, I showed it to my mother, who knew Kimberly and I loved each other deeply, and viewed us as a couple. This could only have been further evidence of our closeness, which she encouraged and facilitated. Tacitly, my father viewed us the same way, for he let me out of his grip whenever I was needed at Kimberly's, or I merely wanted to be with her.

What I was to Jill and Martie is an interesting question. I sat for them and saw them grow. In age, they were much closer to me than I was to their mother. With different parents, I could have been an older brother, which I often acted like. In my pajamas, I lounged on the beds in their room while we watched TV or talked. Sometimes, we had pillow fights, the girls, and occasionally Kimberly, ganging up on me. As we horsed around, a couple of times Jill ended up on my lap getting bounced up and down and shrieking with laughter. The third time it happened, Kimberly came in and stopped it. She took me aside, and quietly, but firmly, admonished me not to do it again.

"Why?" I wanted to know. "Did I do something wrong? Jill seems to enjoy it."

Kimberly looked at me sternly and said, "Johnny, you're wearing only pajamas!"

"Do you think Jill feels something?" I asked.

"Of course she does," Kimberly answered. "Why do you think she's responding this way?"

Given their ages, either of Kimberly's daughters could have become my spouse one day, but I never gave that possibility a thought. In my mind, no one could compete with their mom.

Dick, Steve, and I got along well together. We were friends and serious students who needed no prodding. Most of our interaction while I was in high school came during various sports activities—tennis, touch football, throwing a baseball, or ping pong. Dick and I were on basketball teams at Wakefield. We brothers swam together at the Mountain Place and performed *corvée* for Dad there and at home. In the morning before school, we made a harmonious team in the kitchen preparing breakfast. None of us meddled in each other's business, or had any overlap in social affairs. Dick and Steve knew Kimberly well, but neither had any inkling of what she and I were doing.

In September 1958, my youngest brother, Charlie, started first grade about a quarter of a mile from our house. In the afternoon, when I had no practice or games, I often went to meet him and walk him home. This little brother of mine was a cutie who, like me, loved Kimberly, Jill, and Martie. Whenever they came over, he was always right there, never wanting to miss a thing. However, despite our age difference of almost eleven years, Charlie felt competitive toward me. That I could go off to Fairlington with Kimberly and her girls, but he could only visit them when he was with our mother, rankled him.

One afternoon, Kimberly came to the house to pick me up to go shopping. Mother was out, but Dick and Steve were there. I told Charlie that Kimberly and I had to take care of some business and he had to stay home with our brothers. Charlie would have none of that. In fact, he put on such a temper tantrum and so clung to us that we had no choice but to take him along, and consequently accomplished nothing. All of his pent-up frustration at being unable to do what his oldest brother could do  came out that unforgettable day. I wasn't at all pleased, but had to feel for someone who, like me, was trying to be a person his age wouldn't permit.

## 20  Senior Year

During the first semester of my senior year of high school I was busy with course work, basketball, and applying to college. I spent weekdays with my parents and brothers in our north Arlington home, but unless something interfered, I went on weekends to my other home in Fairlington. We were all students in the latter, Kimberly taking night classes for her B.A., Jill in the sixth grade and Martie in the fourth. When we could, Kimberly and I studied together up in the den.

On a Saturday in early October, former Fairlington neighbors took me with them to Princeton to watch a football game and visit their son, a senior there. They knew from my mother I was interested in applying to Princeton and thought it would be a good way for me to see something of college life. The Princeton scene impressed me, but not the football game.

Unfortunately, Princeton figured in my disastrous basketball season that year, when I was slated to be a starter on the varsity team. Practice began at the end of October; Coach Robinson was planning to have our first intra-team scrimmage several weeks later. By coincidence, this scrimmage and an after-school visit from a Princeton representative to meet with prospective students were scheduled for the same hour, so I told Mr. Robinson well in advance I would be late for practice.

The day of the meeting, several other seniors and I waited around for the Princeton man, only to hear he'd been delayed and would have to come another time. Seeing me enter the gym in my coat and tie when the team had already warmed up and was on the court ready to begin, Coach Robinson pounced on me.

"John, you're late!" he said. "Where've you been? Practice started forty minutes ago! I guess you're not interested enough in the team to play first-string."

I was astounded to hear this, which was patently false, and said in response, "I told you last week I'd be late for practice today. Have you forgotten?" He had, but was unwilling to concede the point.

I quickly dressed and came upstairs, but found I was now on the second team. That incident so soured my coach's mind that I never had a chance to prove him wrong.

Despite my unhappiness, I remained on the squad, and played as a frequent sub. I hated being sent in cold to try to salvage a difficult situation. By the time I got limbered up and started to get in a groove, I found myself back on the bench until the next unpleasant episode.

Unlike previous years, I also felt much more tired and stressed during these games. I was working hard on my studies and going to bed late. Sometimes, my weekend activities at Kimberly's added to this fatigue. The only satisfaction I had the entire season came one day during practice, when the coach called us over for a strategy session. As my teammates took their seats facing the coach in one section of the pull-down bleachers, I went to another section close by. Seeing this, the team co-captains, Scotty, being one of them, jumped up, came over, and sat down beside me. At this blatant show of loyalty toward a player who thought more of his academic future than basketball, Mr. Robinson got red in the face and grimaced in surprise and consternation, his wrinkled nose lifting his wire-rimmed glasses up toward his furrowed brow.

The rides home this vindictive coach and neighbor of mine gave me after practice and games were mostly silent affairs. Before he went from the varsity to the JV squad, my brother, Dick, came along, too. Mr. Robinson dubbed us "the scholars" because we always had a book to read on the way to a game or while waiting around after practice. My coach could never figure me out or forgive what he considered my peculiar attitude.

Perhaps his view of me was colored as well by my relationship with Kimberly. He saw her in the stands and waiting for me after games, when I asked for permission to ride home with her and the girls. No doubt, he also heard rumors, which fed his curiosity. How strong this was became clear when our coach asked my brother prying questions about Kimberly and me on the way to practice one day. Dick was totally unaware of our love life, and found this inquisitiveness offensive. Mr.

Robinson wasn't alone in wanting to know. Two of our Wakefield cheerleaders, one of them Bobbi Coulter, with whom I opened our seventh grade dance, once asked Dick, "What's wrong with us in your brother's eyes?"

Before the fiasco with Coach Robinson the day of the canceled meeting with the Princeton representative, I went with my father to his alma mater, Haverford College, for an interview and tour of the campus. The first time I visited Haverford was in the spring of 1954, when Dad took Dick, Steve, and me along to his fifteenth reunion. Now I was back as a prospective freshman. With an enrollment of a bit over four hundred male students, Haverford had become somewhat larger than in 1939 when my father graduated, but its academic standards were as high as ever and its Quaker affiliation still strong.

My interview with Bill Ambler, the Director of Admissions, started at ten on a weekday morning in his Roberts Hall office. A short, stocky man with a ruddy complexion, he was a Haverford graduate who played football in his day, and was always happy to find an applicant who could participate in collegiate athletics. Haverford, as I later experienced, was a "grind" school where varsity level sports were appreciated but not overly emphasized. The fact that my father and his older brother were Haverford alumni carried considerable weight.

While Dad sat beside me, Mr. Ambler reviewed my academic record and talked with me about my athletic experience.

Then, he asked, "What do you want out of college?" a question for which I wasn't prepared. Going to college was a given in my mind, as it was for most in the Wertime clan.

Not sure what to say, I answered, "I want to work hard and learn as much as I can."

After this exchange, Mr. Ambler looked at me and said with a smile, "Shall I save a place for you in next year's freshman class?"

I was floored by his question, but quickly recovered, and said, "Yes, please."

As we left Roberts Hall, I was in a daze and uncertain of the meaning of Mr. Ambler's final question and offer.

"What was he after when he asked what I want out of college?"

I queried Dad.

"I think he was looking for an answer such as 'I want a college education in order to grow as a person,'" Dad said.

Then I asked my father, "What do you think my chances are of getting in?"

"Well," he said, "Bill Ambler asked you if he should save a place for you in next year's freshman class. As far as I can see, you've been admitted."

That helped put my mind at ease, but I wasn't fully convinced this was the case until I received a formal letter of admission in the spring.

Before setting out for home, we attended a couple of classes, walked around the campus, and looked briefly at Haverford's nature walk.

Kimberly was happy to hear about my meeting with Mr. Ambler, but was distressed by what happened with my basketball coach. Because of her Massachusetts connection and what I'd heard about Amherst, I thought I should look into that college as well. Regarding Amherst, she said to me, "Johnny, if you're really interested in going there, you should see the campus and have an interview. My brother-in-law's an Amherst man, and can arrange a meeting for you." I agreed, and soon was on my way with Kim and the girls to her sister's for the Thanksgiving holiday and a visit to Amherst the following day.

For our Thanksgiving meal, Kimberly's sister, Jill, had a big turkey and all the right complements. After I dispatched my first helping, Jill offered me seconds, then thirds. For someone with a hollow leg to pass up this opportunity, especially when an appreciative cook urges you on, would have been both impolitic and impolite, I thought. I thus ended up eating half their turkey that day, and established my reputation as a trencherman in their family, as it was in mine.

The interview I had at Amherst was cordial enough, but later I heard from Kimberly the people there thought I really wanted to go to Haverford or Princeton, and weren't keen on being a third choice, so I didn't apply.

Before the end of autumn, I had my Princeton interview and

submitted an application for early admission. The word that came in January was negative, so I waited for an official letter from Haverford. In the end, this all worked out well. The very liberal, non-conformist atmosphere of Haverford was perfect for me. Importantly, too, it was the closest of all three colleges to Kimberly.

On Christmas Eve, my family, including my father and Grandma Schultz, went to Kimberly's home for eggnog and cookies. Dad rarely did anything like that. This may even have been his first time in Kimberly's home. Why he came along that evening I can't say. Perhaps he wanted to see the radiant Kimberly, or the place where I was spending so much of my time. Mother, Dick, Charlie, and I attended the St. Clement's Christmas Eve service with the Blakes. Holding mistletoe mischievously over her head afterward, Kimberly called me to her for an opportunity that rarely came in public.

 During the Christmas vacation, I spent as much time with Kim as I could spare. I had basketball practice and research to do at the Library of Congress, where I went several times using Kimberly's car. Some years earlier, I visited that great library with my father, and went again with him to refamiliarize myself. He had a carrel where he kept library books for his research, and even had a pass to get into the stacks. The main reading room at that time of year was full of college and high school students working on term papers due after the Christmas break.

New Year's Eve wasn't a special occasion in our house. Dad did then what he did most nights—read, write, or practice his violin or viola. Mother followed her usual routine of making dinner, cleaning up, and typing for Dad, or joining him in playing a sonata. We brothers read, played ping pong or a game like Monopoly with or without our parents, and listened to music in our rooms. We watched no TV, because Dad thought it was a waste of time and wouldn't have one in the house. Thanks to Kimberly, I found something better to do on the eve of 1959, when we welcomed in the New Year on our nocturnal bed in her living room.

One of the Wertime family activities during the cold winters of the 1950's was ice skating on the C & O Canal that runs along the Maryland side of the Potomac River. Early in January, Kimberly, Jill, and Martie joined us there for some nighttime fun. Dick was our best skater, having played ice hockey for a while. I called him "Rocket Richard" after one of hockey's greats. Steve, too, skated well. My parents and youngest brother were all good on the ice, as was Kimberly, with her background in the northern part of New York state. Jill and Martie were still beginners, but I was the one most at risk on skates and prone to bone-jarring falls. With good reason, our coach warned his players to stay off the ice during basketball season. The previous year when our team made it to the state finals, I heeded his advice. But the way things were going my senior year, it didn't matter to me anymore.

Toward the end of January, there was so much snow that Arlington schools were closed for a week. I was at my parents' home when the great storm hit. Dick was in Fairlington and ended up staying at Kim's. To miss some school was not so bad because I had plenty of homework and research to do. For the first few days, I kept busy reading and shoveling snow, but as the week wore on, I got more and more frustrated at not being able to get where I wanted to be. Finally, the roads were plowed just enough for mother to pick up my brother and drop me off. While Dick didn't get the treatment I got there, he, too, knew the pleasure of staying in Kimberly's home.

On my first night back with Kimberly and the girls, we grabbed our sleds and joined the adults and children on the long hill behind my old elementary school. First holding Jill, then Martie, I scooted downward lickety-split with Kimberly and a daughter following close behind. Sometimes, too, Kimberly and I rode together, or I followed her down. I still can see her rosy nose and cheeks glowing in the cold moonlit night as we climbed up the hill.

In late February, the regular basketball season ended and Wakefield was preparing to play in the Northern Virginia Regional Tournament. Over the long George Washington Birthday holiday weekend, I came down with a fever and cold at Kimberly's house. To protect the three of them, I moved over to my grandmother's place. Still too sick to go to our morning practice, I passed by Kimberly's house on my way to buy some medicine in the Fairlington Shopping Centre. A teammate of mine who lived nearby, evidently spotted me and told Mr. Robinson.

As I entered the locker room to dress for a scrimmage once back in school, the coach confronted me with the whole team looking on.

"John," he said, "why didn't you come to the holiday practice?"

"I was sick," I answered.

"That's not what I heard," Mr. Robinson replied. "Someone said he saw you going to your girlfriend's house."

"That's not true!" I responded angrily. "I was staying at my grandmother's and walked to the drug store to get some medicine!"

Despite my valid explanation, my coach didn't believe me. Then he gave me an ultimatum. "If you want to remain on the team," he said, "you'll have to sit in the stands in your street clothes during the first game of the tournament. After you've practiced again, you can dress and sit on the bench."

Humiliated by this treatment, I suddenly said, "I quit!"

I immediately gathered up my practice gear, turned in my uniform, and left with the same feeling of bitterness I started with in mid-November.

With the basketball season over prematurely, and having no particular interest in playing baseball again, I was free of sports in the spring for the first time since I was ten. Delectable opportunities now arose. A couple of times a week, Kimberly parked along a side street near Wakefield and waited for me to leave school. I looked for her green station wagon, slipped into the vacant driver's seat, and headed for home, where our quiet mid-week dalliance started about two-thiry, when the girls were still in school. Mindful of our limited time, Kimberly wore a skirt and was ready for me.

Unlike basketball, I never needed any warmup to start this game. Kimberly didn't need much, either. We had the ride home from Wakefield to touch and talk, so we were set to go. Both bedrooms were available then, or if we preferred, there was the toilet seat, where I sat and my lover straddled me. Standing up straight at the top of the stairs was another pleasure. At the door when the girls arrived, Kimberly told them, as I greeted them, too, "Johnny just dropped by to say a quick hello. After your snack, we'll drive him home." Unlike our late night trysts, these afternoon intermezzos refreshed and energized me until well after dark.

Some mornings before I left to catch the bus, we went to the basement for a quick goodbye. Kimberly would lean forward over a table and I'd mount her from behind. We didn't try every position the *Kama Sutra* described, but experienced enough to add extra flavor to our lovemaking and keep it from becoming routine.

On such a morning, when I was back in school and chatting with Scotty, I briefly let down my guard concerning these extra-curricular activities. To my less experienced classmate, who often asked about "my woman," I offered this advice: "The best time to have sex is early in the morning."

Hearing this, Scotty looked at me in wide-eyed astonishment, and exclaimed, "Is that so?"

What Scotty made of my advice at the time, I didn't know, but many years later, he reminded me of what I told him that morning, after which he said, once again, "I want to know about that woman of yours!"

I was a loner who got along well with those I knew. I didn't have a lot of friends or need the company of many. All I required was the love of one. Kimberly was that special person to me. She excited and fulfilled me sexually; I did the same for her. She was my intimate companion, one I looked to for guidance and wisdom. In turn, I provided companionship and a feeling of protection to her and her girls.

That spring, Kimberly revealed how deeply she felt about me. On the second finger of her left hand, next to a ring that had been her mother's, she had placed a new wedding band to complement the signet ring she had given me. Kimberly knew what it meant to be married. Now she wore a visible sign of her true affection for me. I loved her as my wife. Only we two knew how close we were, how deep our improbable love ran. On April ninth, I became eighteen; nine days later, Kimberly turned thirty-six. This gap was something that wouldn't go away, however hard we wished it. Until it caught up with us, we were too busy living and loving to pay attention to this unpleasant fact.

Time I once spent on the baseball field I now devoted to Kimberly. One afternoon when we were together, she asked me to watch a film with her in the auditorium of Fairlington School. I was happy to do this, but was curious to know what it was about. "Breast cancer," she said. If she had made this request of me the previous year, I probably would have been too embarrassed to go. Now I was more mature and ready to do anything I could for her. The response to this new type of educational film was overwhelming. We had to wait in a long line to get into the auditorium, where I appeared to be the only male. The film was frank for the time, showing a woman with bare breasts and how to do a self-examination. Cancer ran in Kimberly's family. Her mother died of it, as did her husband and her sister's twelve-year-old daughter.

The makers of the new Polaroid camera were pushing hard to publicize it in the spring of 1959. To demonstrate this product, they hired attractive young women, who needed only a camera, film, and brochures to do the job. Desiring some extra pocket money, Kimberly signed up for $15-a-day plus ownership of the camera upon completion of her assignments. The first of these was at a fair in Towson, Maryland, a couple of hours from Fairlington. I drove Kimberly there on a Saturday morning and spent the day watching her hand out literature and snapping pictures to show passersby. She also took photos of me at the fair and at home with the leftover film.

The next morning, Kimberly was sick for the first time since I had known her. She came down with a bad case of the flu and couldn't get out of bed. It was almost surreal, seeing her stretched out that way. She was always the healthy, smiling one, full of vim and vigor, standing over her girls or me when we were tired, sick, or feeling blue. Seeing her in this condition, I remembered how I felt as a child staring at my sick mother. Now it was my turn to play nurse and try to help ease her pain. I brought her medicine and water, then lay down beside her and held her the way I did before we made love. She was too sick for anything that smacked of that, so I had to restrain myself and keep a respectful distance.

Unable to go to Baltimore for her next assignment, she asked my mother to take her place. Mother rode the bus to Union Station in Washington, then the train to Baltimore. This continued throughout the week.

Kimberly worked hard as a history major, earning straight A's in her courses. In an anthropology course she took, the subject of authority in primitive societies came up. The solution one of these groups hit upon fascinated her. "It was," she told me with glee, "the man with the largest genitals who became chief." Kimberly's professors were impressed with her work (I was sure she also charmed them), and encouraged her to think of continuing on for a master's when she completed her undergraduate degree. One spring day, she took me along to a class.

Sometimes, Kimberly and I went to Washington to shop, see a movie, or just look around. While we sat in a coffee shop having a snack one morning, a young black woman slipped into our booth and plopped down beside me, much to our surprise. I had no idea what was going on in her mind or what she wanted from us. She wished us good day, then babbled incoherently with a strange, faraway look in her eyes. Kimberly whispered we should be careful of her, then asked a waitress to get the woman out, but to no avail. A few minutes later, the woman got up of her own accord, wished us a good day again, and left. As I looked at Kimberly quizzically, she said, "Johnny, let's go!" We paid the bill and were going out the door when Kim told me the woman was most likely high on heroin.

The mother of Kimberly's college roommate lived close by in Parkfairfax. "Mother Byrd," as Kimberly called her, worked for years in the Capitol Hill office of an Alabama congressman. On several of her visits to this gracious southern lady, she took me with her. I always got along well with older women, and Mother Byrd was no exception. Kimberly's own mother had passed away. Her roommate's mother helped fill a gap in her life.

Of the 415 students in my senior class, I ranked fourteenth at graduation. Most of us went on to college. During study hall my last semester, several of my classmates and I frequently used this free period to discuss all kinds of things. The taste for discussion and debate these sessions kindled in me carried over into my freshman year of college.

During final exams, I was astounded to learn that two of my peers had recently gotten married and were expecting a child. Other than what I saw or heard in class or on one of my teams, I really didn't know much about my fellow students. Whatever else may have been the case, I thought one thing was true—no others at school were in a relationship at all like mine.

The biggest social event of the year, the senior prom, like all other school dances or private parties, meant nothing to me. Kimberly knew from her own high school days how important the prom was for most students. A couple times, I heard her say, "Johnny, I'm sorry you're going to miss this experience. I had such a good time at my prom. I wish you could, too."

For the graduation ceremony in the school gymnasium, each student was allotted three tickets. I wanted Kimberly to have one of them, but she refused to go in place of Grandma Schultz.

## 21 Lucky Find

Thanks to a tip from a friend, I landed a good paying summer job as one of two directors of a small playground in Parkfairfax, a fifteen-minute walk from Kimberly's home. The man who hired me also hired his younger brother as the other director. Our responsibilities were minimal. We had to open, close, and supervise a facility consisting of a fenced-in play area, a few swings, sand box, pavilion, and stationary spring-loaded rides. When we arrived in the morning, we put out some chairs near a covered picnic table, policed the area, and kept an eye on the children who came to play or hang out. Once in a while, the playground got a bit crowded, but usually there weren't many patrons and, when it rained, none at all. On such days, we got paid for reading or loafing.

The playground's proximity to Fairlington provided a rationale for spending time at Kimberly's, or if needed, at my grandmother's house. Otherwise, I had to get a ride to and from work. For lunch, my colleague or I usually walked to the nearby Hot Shoppe in Shirlington for a takeout burger, milkshake, and fries. Later that summer, some of the older kids who spent time with us mentioned an inexpensive fast food restaurant that had recently opened in the area, one I hadn't heard of before. Together, we walked to a place called "McDonald's," where hamburgers were a quarter apiece and the French fries were fabulous. My playground job was a lucky find. I was able to be in Fairlington a good part of the summer and save up for college in the fall.

A child who often came to play was a six-year-old boy called Charlsey. He was a handsome kid with a highly attractive mother. One of the older boys who saw me staring at her told me she was a model at Garfinkle's, Washington's most exclusive department store. Charlsey's mom was just about the opposite of Kim. She was relatively short, had short dark brown hair, and a Mediterranean complexion. I was impressed by her tightly pinched waist and curvaceous hips. She was svelte and petite, but also rather voluptuous. As hard as I tried, I couldn't keep my eyes off her. Little did I know that one day, I'd marry a young woman who more closely resembled Charlsey's mom than my statuesque Kimberly.

Around nine-thirty on a warm, dry night late in June, Kimberly came downstairs to the living room, where I was reading. I noticed she was wearing a skirt instead of her usual Bermuda shorts, but didn't think much of it at the time.

"Johnny," she said, "Jill and Martie are upstairs watching TV and will be okay by themselves for a while. Let's take a short stroll."

That sounded good to me, so out we went, and headed down 36th Street toward Shirley Highway. The air was fresh, and aromatic, too, thanks to Kimberly's perfume. Walking tall and straight beside me, she made me feel happy to be alive. With no one in sight, Kimberly grasped my hand, something she'd never done in our community before. Soon, we arrived at the end of the street, where it curves to join 34th. Opposite this quiet spot was a tiny park, with a bench facing us. "Let's sit over there awhile," Kimberly proposed.

By the time we reached the empty bench, the shining moon and summer air had worked their magic on us. In a fit of passion, with caution to the wind, we grabbed each other in a torrid embrace, right there in our own neighborhood. What came next far surpassed any reveries I'd ever had. While hugging and kissing excitedly, Kimberly nudged me backwards onto the bench. Then she opened my fly and reached inside. Seeing I was fully erect and hard as a rock, she was ready with her surprise.

She suddenly rose up in front of me and hoisted up her skirt. All this time, she'd been naked underneath and dripping with desire. My eyes bugged out at such a sight, and my heart palpitated wildly, but I knew what to do. First glancing up and down the street for any sign of life, I pulled my pants down below my knees, then Kimberly swiftly mounted me for the ride of her life.

Sitting on her bucking bronco, her legs wrapped tightly around mine, she bounced up and down in excitement, heightened by our bold enterprise. Unlike most rodeo riders, she stayed with me to the end, watching me quiver and shake in pleasure as I gave my last kick and heave. Then she, herself, rode up and over her high mountain with ease.

When the show was over, there was no applause, our only spectators being the moon and the stars. But that didn't matter. She had tamed her rambunctious steed. Holding her hand as we headed home, I floated on air beside the woman I loved.

As during the previous summer, I went out with Kimberly and the girls to the movies and to various attractions beyond the suburbs. One place Kim and I went to alone was on the Virginia side of the Potomac River, well above Great Falls. There, in water that was still reasonably clean, one could canoe or even swim. The current was swift, so many people used inner tubes. In the middle of the river, not far below the boat rental dock, were several small islands. We paddled our canoe from one to another, until we found a suitable spot to disembark. Being alone on a deserted island presented unexpected opportunities. There was just one problem—Kimberly wasn't prepared. Our hugging and kissing got me excited, so my left-handed lover did what she enjoyed doing to relieve the pressure I felt.

In early July, Kimberly set off with Jill and Martie for summer camp. I pined away for them at home and at the Parkfairfax playground, but would see them in three weeks. I wouldn't be the only Wertime there, for Kimberly had hired my brother, Dick, to be a camp counselor.

When I arrived, the old campers were gone and the new ones hadn't come in. My first floor quarters in the large building on the hill put me closer to Kimberly than I was the previous summer, a direct reflection of our evolving relationship. I saw my seventeen-year-old brother several times during this short visit, but given the preoccupations each of us had, our encounters were brief. He introduced me to some of the female counselors, all of whom were older than us, but I had no reason to be interested in them. Dick enjoyed the work and companionship at the retreat. I believe he also found romance there, as I certainly did.

Besides seeing Kim and her children, the great pleasure of the retreat for me was walking among its lofty trees and across its spacious lawns. The two crystal-clear days I happened to be there proved perfect for both of these. While the girls were swimming and playing, Kim and I wandered about the campus, talking away. At night, when they were asleep, we went outside to see the moon and stars lighting up the sky and trees. In the warm, gentle breeze, we lay down on the grass to enjoy the spectacular sight, but soon found ourselves gazing at each other, hugging, and kissing. Kimberly was ready, and made love with me on the lush green grass, with little thought of being seen. I returned at the end of the final session to help pack up and drive them home.

During the summer of '59, a defrocked Spanish priest mysteriously appeared in Virginia and was flirting with the Episcopalians. Toward the end of August, a person in the Diocesan center in Richmond called Kimberly for help. They were interested in this man and wanted someone to show him around Washington and Alexandria, where the Virginia Theological Seminary was only a few minutes from her house.

On a hot, humid night, I drove the three of us in Kimberly's car to the Jefferson Memorial along the Tidal Basin. Carlos, a big, dark haired and dark skinned man, was greatly moved by the statue of Jefferson standing alone under a dome similar to those he designed for Monticello and the University of Virginia. Our guest explained that in Spain, it was common for people to express strong emotions in public places by some sort of verbal gesture. He wondered if it would be all right to do the same in Washington. Kimberly said she thought that would be fine, so Carlos stepped back, inhaled deeply, cupped his hands to his mouth, and shouted, "Viva Jefferson!"

For years, the stretch of road along Route 7 between North Fairlington and Bailey's Crossroads remained undeveloped. In a now fully built-up area of high-rises called Skyline, there was at different times a small airport with searchlights, drive-in theater, golf driving range, and even a gypsy camp. My brother, Steve, when he was no more than ten, went from there on his first airplane ride with a neighbor who flew a piper cub. During my high school years, a traveling carnival occupied this spot for a week in late summer. One night, I borrowed Kimberly's car to visit it.

Besides the usual rides, games, food, and prizes, I found a man promoting a side show featuring a hermaphrodite. Shouting "Come see him and her in the same body" for those who didn't know what a hermaphrodite was, he succeeded in selling a lot of tickets. We early customers went inside the tent and milled about in front of a small stage. The tent soon filled with men, most of whom were older than me, and a few women. When his tickets were sold, the barker came in and ordered men to move to the left and women to the right, then pulled a curtain between us. While waiting around for the hermaphrodite to appear, some of the men started to cut up and several became alarmingly rowdy. Suddenly, all fell still when we saw a person dressed as a female step out of the dark onto the stage.

After the barker made a brief introduction, the woman started to disrobe, showing little emotion and saying nothing. Her facial features were quite masculine, though, and she had something of a dark, shadowy beard. I saw very small breasts and a hairy belly like that on some paunchy men. When she was fully naked in front, her vulva appeared quite normal. Then came the surprise. She reached up and pulled down a small penis, which dangled in front of us. One of the men piped up in a thick West Virginia accent, "Yep, that's it all right!" Upon hearing this, the subdued male crowd let out a loud laugh and the show was soon over. Before we reached the exit, the handful of women on the other side of the curtain had vanished into the night. When I got back to the house, Kimberly asked me what I had seen and done. I told her about this pathetic show.

Dad and me at home in Tehran, summer 1962.

# Part III — *Cognizance*

## 22 Separation

Public schools in Arlington opened the Tuesday following Labor Day. Not being in class that morning after twelve years felt strange. I was happy to have more time with Kimberly, but was conflicted. The thing I both looked forward to and dreaded the most was rapidly approaching—new students at Haverford were to arrive Wednesday, September sixteenth. I told Kimberly how much I loved her and how anguished I felt about our coming separation. In the way I looked and acted, she could see this was true. Due to bitter experience or more self-control, Kimberly knew how to hide her emotions better than I. In fact, she used to tell me, "My dear, you'll never make a good liar or spy. Whatever you feel inside you shows clearly on your face!"

Kimberly tried to assure me everything would be okay. To cheer me up, she would say, "College will be a great learning experience, one that'll change your life." A couple of times, I also heard, "You'll meet a pretty college girl who'll steal your heart." However hard Kim attempted to hide it, I could see distress in her face as well. She was right about college being a great learning experience and changing my life, but one of the ways it did this neither of us anticipated.

As the first of four brothers to go to college, I was feeling my way. The $700 I saved from summer work went toward my fall tuition. With Mother's and Kimberly's help, I set about getting items I needed to take along. One thing we bought was a laundry box, in which I could mail my dirty clothes home and get them back washed and ironed. Well before the sixteenth, I had everything ready to go.

In the days preceding my departure, Kimberly and I clung to each other and made love as often as we could. I tried to comfort her and myself by suggesting we communicate by some sort of mental telepathy. "When you're lonely and thinking of me," I said, "go look at the moon and know, I'll be outside looking at it, too, and thinking of you."

My last night at Kimberly's home before I left for college was particularly poignant. I wasn't going off to war as her late husband had done, but the trauma of separation was no less real. We promised to write each other regularly and call whenever possible. How used to, and dependent on, each other we were was now clearer than ever. I didn't know how I'd survive this without her presence.

"Johnny," Kimberly told me, "once classes have started, you'll be so busy you'll soon forget me."

"That's not true!" I replied. "I'll never forget you, Kim!"

Kimberly also had classes of her own to attend. She spoke of having to keep busy with studying to make the time go by faster until my return at Thanksgiving.

On Wednesday the sixteenth, I said goodbye to my father and brothers before they left the house for work and school. Later that morning, Kimberly drove over to pick up Mother and me for the trip to Haverford. I was both happy and sad to leave my two homes and families behind.

When we arrived in front of Barclay Hall, the freshman dorm, upperclassmen were stationed outside ready to assist. I had a letter telling me I would be on the second floor in 221 with Paul Moyer and Jerry Darlington. Kimberly and Mother unloaded the car while student helpers and I ran my few possessions upstairs. Paul and Jerry were already there. After I introduced myself, my mother, and my secret lover, we looked around Barclay, then went downstairs to park the car and take a brief tour of the campus. Before they left, I hugged and kissed both Mother and Kim, but was careful not to favor the latter for fear of giving our secret away. Then I saw them drive down the long lane towards the duck pond and Lancaster Avenue. Mother later remarked how sad I looked as I stood watching them go. What I imagine was a happy experience for my new classmates was bittersweet for me.

After their departure, I returned to Barclay to settle in and get acquainted with my roommates. The three of us had a two-bedroom suite with a sitting room in the middle. Paul arrived first and occupied the single room. Jerry was in the room with the double-decker bed, which left me in a quandary—how to occupy a small bedroom with another person given my need for privacy. Full of apprehension as I was putting my things away, I heard Paul say, "If this arrangement doesn't suit every-one, please let me know."

No words were more welcome than those and I immediately re-sponded, "I'm not used to sharing a room. If you're willing to trade places, I'd be most grateful." Paul graciously agreed and moved in with Jerry while I transferred my things to my new quarters. Our agreement was for the first semester, but Paul let me stay on for the year. He took the desk in the sitting room and Jerry the one in their shared bedroom. Without Paul's kindness, I don't know what my freshman year of col-lege would have been like. Sitting at his desk throughout the next nine months, Paul was always cordial as Jerry and I entered and left our suite.

After sorting things out and arranging our rooms, we joined our fellow freshmen for our first meal in Founders Hall, the oldest building on campus. The dining room there, with its tall windows and high walls, on which portraits of Haverford notables hung, made a long lasting im-pression.

With the old students' return, I quickly learned about the Col-lege's traditions. The first one startled me. To welcome a young female guest to dinner during the week, students banged their spoons and knives loudly on the tabletops and metal pitchers. Our mates also used this time to tell jokes and funny stories, or raise an issue of relevance to the college community. Campus wits abounded. The cartoons, limericks, montages and other forms of diabolical humor they posted on Founders bulletin boards kept us entertained and sometimes, in stitches. Not long into the first year of Hugh Borton's undynamic presidency, one of them sized him up and dubbed him "Huge Abortion."

My faculty advisor was Gerald Freund, a Haverford and Oxford graduate, who taught political science. I took introductory courses with him both semesters and intermediate French with Brad Cook, another outstanding teacher. In freshman English, a mandatory class, we all read the same novel per week and wrote a paper on it for presentation in a small tutorial. My professor and tutor, James Harper, was the best per-son I could have had. No course I took at Haverford proved to be of more lasting benefit.

146

As the semester got underway, I engaged in ongoing discussions with various residents of my corridor, the closest one of whom was my roommate Paul. I was far to the left of him socially and sexually, so we seldom agreed on anything. Terry Belanger and Jacques Transue, who roomed together nearby, were also part of my small coterie of debating friends. In 2005, Terry would win a MacArthur "genius" award for his work in rare books.

Those were fun times. Unfortunately, they didn't last beyond the first half of the year. I had to work harder and harder to make my mark, and didn't find time to engage in extra-curricular activities that would have put me in closer touch with more of my interesting classmates. Working late at night, I usually took a break around ten for a milkshake at the snack bar in the basement of the Student Union.

At dusk, before I went to dinner, I headed to the soccer field to grieve at my separation from Kimberly. While sitting alone on the bleachers and staring at the orange and light blue autumn sky, I thought of my loved one and her girls far away in Virginia. Often, too, I sought solace in the nature walk that surrounded part of the campus.

During my first months at Haverford, I wrote to Kimberly several times a week, and she to me. In our letters, we were quite open in expressing our feelings for each other. When I could, I called her from the public telephone down the corridor from my room. Sometimes, around nine-thirty at night, someone would knock on the door of our suite to inform me that I had a call. I rushed to the phone, hoping to hear Kimberly's voice. Most often, it was she, asking how I was, and telling me how much they all missed me.

As in high school, I had no interest in socializing with my female peers. There were plenty of them a mile away at Bryn Mawr, and even closer at Harcum Junior College and two private girls' prep schools. Many of my classmates lost no time in visiting our sister college, and inviting its students to Barclay for parties or more intimate affairs. My loneliness, I knew, would end during vacations. Besides, my life had been this way since Kimberly and I first became lovers, only now, the intervals between our unions had grown longer. I worked hard like a monkish scholar. My need for sex was related only to her. I was loyal to the woman I loved like a wife, and couldn't imagine being attracted to any other.

In a lecture I attended at Bryn Mawr in the middle of November, I heard about a modern Jewish philosopher's thoughts on relationships, which got me thinking about Kimberly and me. In his treatise, *I and Thou*, Martin Buber maintained there are two types of relationships between human beings and the world: "I-It" and "I-Thou." The former is imperfect and impersonal. It is the normal everyday relationship of a human being with the things surrounding him, including other humans. In an "I-It" relationship, others are viewed from a distance, like a thing, and as part of the environment. The partners in this relationship aren't equal. This, Buber says, is a necessary relationship that leads to objective knowledge.

The "I-Thou" relationship, on the other hand, is radically different. It is direct, mutual, and open, a true dialogue; both sides speak as equals and enter it with their innermost and whole being. The latter, I thought, described the love between Kimberly and me.

Thanksgiving vacation started on Wednesday, November twenty-fifth, when my last class ended at noon. Excited to be going home, I had to hurry through lunch, grab my suitcase and books, and walk fast to the Haverford Station, where I boarded the Paoli Local bound for Thirtieth Street in Philadelphia. From there, I caught a southbound train packed with other college students. I had learned and experienced a great deal in those first two months that passed like a flash as well as an eternity. Kimberly was right in what she told me. College was making me a different person in important respects, save in one—my devotion to her.

I wanted Kim to meet me at Union Station in Washington and take me home to Fairlington. She agreed to pick me up, but insisted she drive me directly to my family, because, she said, "They'll be hurt if you're not with them tonight and tomorrow, after being away so long. We'll have time together, but you've got to be patient until I come to pick you up. How does Friday after lunch sound?"

At home with my parents and brothers, there was much to talk about. As I held forth at the dinner table that evening, Dad listened more than he usually did before taking over with an account of his own affairs

148

and ideas about the world. Mother was particularly happy to see me and was her dependably kind and cheery self. I chatted with my brothers and heard something of their lives. Grandma Schultz came the next day to help Mother prepare our Thanksgiving meal, while we males played football, then took a walk.

When Kimberly and I were together on Friday, I was eager to tell her about Martin Buber's philosophy. I explained how I thought our relationship had the qualities he described as being of the "I-Thou" type. Then I suggested we engrave the inside of our rings with "I-Thou" to show our closeness.

"That's a good idea," Kimberly said, "but what if someone sees this and gets wind of our relationship?"

"Well," I responded, "let's put it in French," to which she agreed. Kimberly knew no French, so when I unthinkingly wrote down an infelicitous *moi-tu* instead of *moi-toi* for the engraver, she didn't know the difference. Before I went back to Haverford, she returned my ring, newly inscribed, and showed me hers with the same inscription.

Our lovemaking and conversations that weekend were both happy and sad. We spoke of our loneliness and desire for each other, and how hard it was to be separated this way. We got caught up on what was going on in our lives and those of the girls. Kimberly had a course with a lot of reading to do. I, myself, had to prepare for a class on Monday morning. Time together, especially unencumbered time, had become a precious commodity.

Riding back to Philadelphia that Sunday afternoon, I experienced once again the bittersweet feeling I had in September. Life had changed for Kimberly and me. This was not the type of commuter love we'd had the year before. Christmas vacation, however, was only three weeks away, something I looked forward to greatly. In the meantime, I had to be content with daydreams of her in my arms.

Haverford's JV basketball season opened at home the first Saturday in December. My roommate, Jerry, and I played the whole game, which we lost by only a basket. I scored seventeen points, the most I'd ever gotten in my basketball career, but the coach blamed the loss on me. At the final buzzer, he ran onto the court and lit into me for something I didn't understand. Had I failed to cover my man? Or was it something else? Exhausted from playing so hard, and proud of my scoring achievement, I was unprepared for his flushed face thrust into mine, and for the tongue lashing he gave me. Perhaps I was too sensitive in general, or hypersensitive when it came to basketball coaches, but that confrontation diminished my zest for the team.

The same evening I was on the Haverford court, an event took place in Virginia that would change my life. What ultimately brought this about was a chance encounter in the early '50s, when my father and friends were playing string quartets in our living room one summer night and befriended Todd Johnson, a passerby who asked to come in and listen.

Todd Johnson, I would learn, was twenty-eight years my senior. He was married and divorced without children. A Ph.D. in international relations, he worked in an Army intelligence unit on Soviet affairs and psychological warfare, where he translated Russian documents and literature, and analyed sensitive data. Todd was widely read, knew several languages, collected various types of art, and appreciated classical music. According to a family friend who knew him well, he was also a bit pretentious. To play at musical soirées in his basement rec room, he invited amateur musicians like my father and his friends, whom he enjoyed showing off to his other guests.

Kimberly played the piano, but she never did for me. She felt embarrassed, she said, by her lack of musical proficiency compared to that of my folks. According to Mother, Kimberly mentioned her interest in music to Dad, who thought she might enjoy Todd's soirée, and suggested she come along with them. When they entered his home the Saturday night I was playing basketball, Todd's eyes nearly popped out at the sight of his unexpected guest, Mother recalled. Wasting no time, he glommed onto the elegant woman who owned my body and soul. Exactly how things developed from there I'm unable to say. No doubt Todd turned on the charm and dangled the advantages of years of accumulated wealth and knowledge in front of Kimberly's eyes.

Present at Todd's that night was another man who profoundly impacted my life. He sat behind my father and was also playing the viola. Between numbers, he leaned over, tapped Dad on the shoulder, and offered him the post of cultural attaché in Tehran. Mother had never seen this person before and didn't know his name, but she realized that he, like Dad, worked at USIA. Thus began my family's connection with the ancient country of Iran, one that has influenced me as much as anything has.

Although our late December break for Christmas was designated a vacation, it constituted more of a respite from classes than from work, for the first semester didn't end until January thirtieth. Many college students used these two weeks as a time to catch up on reading and work on papers.

In our north Arlington home, my father was excited about his pending appointment and posting to Iran, and was already studying up on Iranian history. My familiarity with that country came largely from my sixth grade field trip to the Iranian Embassy in Washington.

When I got to Kimberly's, I told her of my silly mistake in French and the need to change the inscription on our rings. Acting immediately, she took them to a jeweler and got it done. It was then that Kimberly informed me she had met Todd Johnson and was going out with him on dates. Even more alarming to hear was what Todd was beginning to talk about—at the end of the coming summer, he would be joining a university down south, and wanted to take a wife and family along with him. When Kimberly told me these things, she didn't indicate any particular interest or excitement in such a prospect. In fact, she seemed conflicted and sad that it had even happened. Yet, it was important and she told me.

My rival wasn't young, tall, blond, or good-looking like me. He smoked a pipe, was slightly stooped, had a crooked nose and a balding dome. He was, however, highly cultured and well-established in his field. Besides a car and the house he lived in, he no doubt had many possessions and assets. Above all, he was a man with a job that offered security and respectability.

What Kimberly told me shook me to the core and revived my fears of losing her. But like my mother, I was full of wishful thinking and capable of ignoring things I didn't want to hear. Besides, Kimberly and I continued our lives as if nothing was happening between her and Todd. We made love as we always did, she soothed my heart and thrilled me. We were the best of friends. She wore a specially inscribed wedding band dedicated to me. Kimberly was like my wife. I loved her deeply.

In mid-January, Kimberly indicated she wanted to come to see me in Philadelphia on a day we had a night basketball game away from home. Given my rocky relationship with the coach, and knowing I'd have to choose, I met Kimberly at the Thirtieth Street Station and skipped the game. We had a bite of lunch together, then found an inexpensive hotel.

Before we entered, she said, "Johnny, tell the clerk we've just arrived from out of town for a conference, and need a room with two single beds to rest in for a few hours."

"What if they want identification?" I asked. "What'll we do then?"

"Don't worry about that," Kimberly answered. "They'll be happy to have our money." Though I felt self-conscious doing this, the clerk didn't bat an eye at my request.

Holding her naked in my arms that day, Kimberly felt and looked somewhat different to me. The taste and tone of her skin had changed, and seemed harder to my fingers and lips. We didn't talk about much of anything. Kim simply needed to be close to me. While in the hotel, she mentioned our rings and said, "I think it best to have the inscriptions erased. Someone could easily find out about us." Who that someone might be she didn't say, and I didn't ask. Without any hesitation, I took off my ring and gave it to her.

Following Kimberly's visit, I dropped off the JV squad to play intramural basketball. Several of my teammates did the same, including Joe Taylor, who would one day become a Nobel laureate in astrophysics. Our two freshmen intramural teams taken together were now as strong as the JV, and a lot more fun.

By the beginning of the second semester, I felt more at ease at Haverford than I had at the beginning of the first, but still missed Kimberly as much as before and counted on her love. In her correspondence and on the phone, I kept hearing about Todd. Kimberly, no doubt, was trying to keep me abreast of things. However, at no point did she come right out and say exactly what was going on in her mind. If she had, what I heard over spring vacation wouldn't have rocked me so. Maybe she herself didn't know until just before that time, or perhaps she did, and wanted to wait to break the news to me in person.

## 23  *Un Printemps Triste*

When I arrived home late Friday afternoon toward the end of March, I found my father studying Persian in preparation for his new job in Tehran. Every day, he attended his small language class at the State Department's Foreign Service Institute not far away in Arlington. He was also reading widely on Persian history and archaeology, and enjoyed talking about such places as Persepolis and Esfahan, and rulers like Cyrus the Great, Darius, Xerxes, Shah Abbas, and Nader Shah.

Sunday night, when I went to stay at Kimberly's, she returned my signet ring with the inscription removed. Despite that, I wore it as I did before.

From the beginning of our intimate relationship, I put myself totally in Kimberly's good hands and trusted her absolutely. She initiated me into sex and love, helped me grow as a lover and companion, indeed, as a person. She educated me in the lessons of life the way Haverford molded me academically. I couldn't imagine living without her. Now, she taught another of life's lessons, one I really didn't want to learn.

Early in the afternoon on Monday, while Jill and Martie were in school, Kimberly called me into the big bedroom and told me to sit down on one of the beds. The look on her face was both serious and sad.

"I have something to tell you, Johnny."

"What's that?" I asked unsuspectingly.

"Todd's asked me to marry him," she stated.

"What did you tell him?" I asked in alarm.

"I told him I would," she answered. Stunned by her response, I started to cry.

"Why did you do that?" I wondered aloud, as tears streamed down my face. By now, Kimberly, too, was crying.

"I had no choice!" she wailed. "I did it for my girls. They're growing up fast. They need a secure future I can't provide by myself."

Now I knew. Financial security and respectability trump all else. In making this decision, Kimberly used her head instead of her heart. I didn't realize it at the time, but besides her girls and herself, she did it for me. What would our lives have been like had she turned down Todd's offer and stuck with me instead?

Kimberly's words hit me like a thunderclap. My head throbbed, and my tears wouldn't stop. Some time went by before I could even talk again.

"Do you love Todd?" I wanted to know.

Having regained her composure, Kimberly put her arms around me and patted me on the back. "There, there," she said in her motherly way, as she had any number of times before. Then she spoke from the heart.

"Johnny, I don't love Todd now. I'll have to learn to love him. I hope he's as good to me as you have been. Johnny dear, we both know that if our ages were closer, you and I would be married now. Unfortunately, God didn't make us so. I'll always love you, but it'll have to be in a different way."

"Kim, I don't want to leave you," I sobbed. "You're the only one I'll ever love!"

Kimberly told me again what she had before, that I was young and just starting out in life, that some day I'd have a beautiful wife and children. She said life would go on for us both, and that she would always love me. But no matter what she said, I couldn't stop my crying. Through no fault of our own, the difference that separated us was insurmountable.

Suddenly, an old image flashed through my mind. Now I knew for certain—the train I'd struggled so hard to catch was pulling away for good, leaving me behind. My worst nightmare had come true. Yet the hardest part was still to come.

I have no idea how long my tears flowed that afternoon. It may have been an hour or more. After a while, Kimberly got up and left the room, but came back to check on me. Each time she looked in, I was still in a state of shock, crying incessantly. Then she sat on the bed and said to me firmly, "Johnny, you've got to get a hold of yourself!"

Nothing she or anyone else could say that day would assuage my sense of desolation. I felt empty inside, as if all the trust I had placed in the safest of hearts had turned to dust. When Jill and Martie were about to come home from school, Kimberly came to me again, held me tight, and told me to go into the bathroom and wash my face so they wouldn't wonder what was going on.

Finally able to stand up, I went to the bathroom to pee and apply a piping hot wash cloth to my eyes. Looking into the mirror, I saw two swollen red spheres staring blankly back at me. Fate had just dealt me a bitter blow. I didn't know how I would survive.

Now that Kimberly had disclosed her secret and cleared the air, what would we do next? She had made a commitment to marry Todd, but didn't break her prior commitment to me. As I lay in bed in the den that night with an aching heart and a befuddled mind, trying to comprehend what had taken place in the afternoon, I heard a soft swishing sound, then felt Kimberly's hand touching mine. "I need to be with you, Johnny," she said. "Will you come downstairs with me?" Despite what had happened that afternoon, I didn't resist or hesitate. She was still mine in my mind, and I, hers if she wanted me. We embraced in our usual spot on the floor as passionately as ever. The nourishment our love making gave me then and during the remainder of my stay, however great, couldn't mitigate the shock that drained me for months to come. That wasn't an auspicious way to enter the age of nineteen.

All spring long, my heart was leaden, as Kimberly's must have been. In telephone conversations and correspondence, she showed none of the enthusiasm one expects of a future bride. In some ways, ours became a life lived in denial, analogous to those informed of a fatal disease and unable to accept the fact. But then, I couldn't forget the sword suspended over my head, like that of Damocles, destined to fall when she married Todd.

In late April or early May, Kim came back to Philadelphia on the train to meet me for the afternoon. Despite the hurt of what I'd been through, I still adored her. What was different now was a certain feel and sense when we made love, one people going off to war must

156

know—that there might be no more—so we clung to each other hard to make our time together last as long as we could.

My anguish notwithstanding, I was able to focus on my studies well enough to finish my first year of college with decent grades. I was lucky to be where I was. There had been no pressure on me to conform or participate in ways that didn't suit me. The curriculum, facilities, and opportunities were as much as I could handle and more than I could take full advantage of. Haverford's extensive lawns and imposing trees soothed my pain. I especially loved the library and the nature walk. When I followed along it, I found the solitude I needed to think of Kimberly. I bore her no grudge or bitterness for what she'd done; it was sadness and hurt that I felt. I couldn't help thinking we'd been born with birthdays out of sync, that fate hadn't been kind to us.

My last exam of the year fell on June first, two days before commencement. By then, my roommates and nearly all the freshmen were gone from Barclay. Walking up and down the silent stairs and through the empty corridors brought a sad and eerie feeling, as if the place had been abandoned, perhaps a premonition of my coming fate. The only thing I heard was the distant sound of a stereo playing Beethoven's Ninth. From the window of my room, I looked out across the emerald-green lawn to the library and two seniors throwing a Frisbee. For the first time since I arrived in mid-September, I was alone in our suite. It was hard to believe the year was already over.

The windows were open wide. The air was fresh and fragrant. I was waiting expectantly for the sound of a motor and the lilt of a special voice. Around twelve forty-five, I finally heard them. I rushed to the window and looked out to see Kimberly standing beside her car. She spotted my face. With a big, beautiful smile and a grand wave of her hand, she cried out, "Johnny, I'm here!"

The sight of Kimberly raised my spirits. She was there by herself to take me home. I ran down to welcome her and bring her up. She was dressed in a tight jean skirt and white blouse. As we walked up the stairs, I grabbed her rear. She gave out a yelp and a lusty laugh. It was a gorgeous spring day, one to delight in and to put sorrows away. When we entered the suite, Kimberly looked around and said, "Johnny, it seems you've thrived here at Haverford. I'm glad you've done so well! I hope everything will continue this way. It's a beautiful place."

I showed her into my room, locked the door, then pulled her to me and rolled on the bed. We hugged and kissed frenziedly until she looked up and said, "Johnny, I need to use the bathroom." I led her down the hall to the one I frequented, and stood on guard outside it. After a couple of minutes, she emerged smiling and prepared. I looked around our suite once more before locking the door. The academic year had ended, and Kimberly would never return. I faithfully observed Haverford's strict honor codes for academics and abstinence from sexual intercourse in its dorms throughout, but on this last day, my love for the woman I was losing took precedence over my pledge.

## 24 Summer of '60

My old job at the Parkfairfax playground was waiting for me when I got back home. The pay was good and the work easy, but there was no excitement to divert my mind from pending doom. During June and the first week of July, up to the time Kimberly and the girls went to camp, I stayed with them, my Grandma Schultz, or with my family, as I had the previous summer.

My father was deep into his Persian and reading on Iran. With Grandma's help, Mother was buying clothes and various household articles in preparation for their three-year sojourn in Tehran. Steve and Charlie were going with them; Dick would be with me at Haverford. After his graduation, he went off to a life-guarding job at a church retreat in the northwestern part of Virginia, thanks to Kimberly's help.

At the playground, I buried myself in books. Among those I read was *Don Quixote*. I did the usual things there and at my parents' home, but everywhere I turned, the rhythm of life was changing. Kimberly and her girls would be leaving soon; my parents and two of my brothers were moving to the Middle East; and Grandma Schultz was talking about pulling up stakes and going to California. My whole support system seemed to be crumbling around me.

There was no one in whom I could confide my grief other than Kimberly herself. However, she was engaged in a struggle of her own and could no longer serve as my confessor or guide. Thus, I had to keep it all bottled up inside me, something she always counseled against.

Kimberly, Jill, and Martie spent more than six weeks at camp. When they returned in mid-August, I was waiting at the door, ready to greet them and help them in for their brief stay in Fairlington. That night, and I think, the next one as well, Kimberly and I made love. But, then, a new attitude took hold of her. She had to get ready for her wedding and move down south. To hear her say, "Johnny, I've got a lot to do. I think it best if you'd stay at Irma's from now on" was another blow to my fragile sense of self. In the way and no longer welcome, I realized my dream of a life with Kimberly was truly ending.

Prior to their departure for Iran, my parents and brothers went out to say goodbye to Dick. The day before Kimberly's wedding, our home in north Arlington now empty, I drove my parents and brothers in our old station wagon to National Airport for the start of their journey. I was sad to see them go, and wouldn't be with them again until the following summer. I gave Mother and Charlie a hug and kiss, Dad and Steve a firm handshake, promised to write, wished them farewell, then returned to my grandmother's house.

On August twenty-third, a minister friend of Kimberly's married her and Todd at St. Clement's. Maurice Hopson was there, but didn't perform the ceremony. He was, I heard, too broken up to do it himself and see the friend he had loved so much leave forever.

As for me, I was nowhere near that church. I wasn't even invited. What would I have done if I'd been there? I might have stepped forward to object to Kimberly's marriage, and said to Todd, "You've got no right to take my wife this way just because you're older and richer than I am! I've loved her with all my heart and might since I was fifteen! I've looked out for her and her girls. We've done many things together and been a family. She and I have made love the way few people ever do. If fate had been kinder, she would be mine. But no matter what you do, I'll always claim her for my own until she lets me go!" Or, maybe I would have broken down and sobbed so loudly no one present could have heard the wedding service. In any case, that terrible dark day sealed my fate. I was brokenhearted and in a frenzy, with no one to confide in or talk to. At the playground, I sat around in a state of shock. I felt I'd been happily married and unwillingly divorced, all by the age of nineteen.

The summer vacation was almost over and the playground about to close. My parents and brothers were on their way to Iran. Grandma

Schultz was still there, but Kimberly would soon be departing. Frantic to know how she was, I had to see Kimberly again. When I knocked on the door. Kim saw my anguish and quickly brought me in. The house looked the same, but things had changed. She was Todd's wife now and had slept with him. When we were able to be alone, I stood before her, tormented and trembling.

"Kim, are you okay?" I asked. "Did Todd treat you well? I hope he didn't hurt you."

Kimberly choked up as she answered me, "Johnny, I'm all right, but it wasn't like being with you. You've always been so kind and gentle with me, something I'll never forget."

After saying that, she began to sob, and took refuge in my arms. Although not by law, she was still all mine in my heart. The love we made that night was an unforgettable one.

Two days later, Kimberly, Jill, and Martie were gone from Fairlington. I was at work when the movers came, and didn't see them go. That was a sight I couldn't bear. After dinner with Grandma Schultz, I walked down the street in a daze to look at the house that had been such an important part of my life. Kimberly and the girls had moved away, taking with them the greatest happiness I had known. Their house stood dark and vacant, the way I felt inside me. For years to come, it would be hard for me to even think about 4229.

The only thing that kept me going was what Kimberly told me just before we parted, "Johnny, I'll write or call you as soon as I can." She gave me their address and telephone number so I could do the same. Todd knew of my father's assignment to Tehran, of my friendship with Kimberly and the girls, and that I would be calling or writing from time to time.

Grandma Schultz felt Mother had deserted her, and was very miffed. To show everyone "she was nobody's fool," she packed up her possessions, called up the movers, and set out for California with her dog. Her abrupt departure came just before my last day of work on September fifth. I drove out to pick up Dick on the sixth. Neither one of us remembers exactly where we went from there. I know I spent a few nights at the home of old Fairlington friends, whose mother was my fourth grade teacher. The back of their home looked across to where

Kimberly had lived. I also recall staying in North Fairlington with my faithful friend, Scotty, and his kind mom and dad.

During this homeless period, I had two goals—to stay in touch with Kimberly, and to show up at Haverford on time to begin my sophomore year of college. On one of my last days in Arlington—it must have been around September tenth—I had an experience that was powerfully moving.

## 25 Reprieve

When I least expected it, Kimberly called me at Scotty's house, told me she had returned to Northern Virginia, and wanted to see me that night. While waiting for her, I thought she still loved me, but didn't know what she had in mind. Just before sundown, she pulled up in an unfamiliar car, wearing her brightest smile. "Johnny, I've missed you!" she said as I got inside. How much she did, I would soon find out.

Riding along, we got caught up on events since her departure. I told her what I knew of my family's trip to Iran, of picking Dick up, and of my grandmother's fit of pique and move out West. Kimberly filled me in on their new house and neighborhood, the girls and their schools, Todd's teaching job, and what she'd seen of life in a southern city.

I didn't know where we were headed until she parked in front of a house which she said belonged to Todd. By now, it was dark outside, and inside the house, even darker. As we approached the front door, Kimberly pulled out a key and opened it. We walked in, turned on an overhead light, and looked around. All the furniture was gone. The only things left on the first floor were the wall-to-wall carpeting, household appliances in the kitchen, and a stereo set and records Todd had planned to take back with them in a day or two. Then we descended a short flight of stairs to the rec room, the scene of the musical soirée where Todd and Kimberly first met. Convinced no one was there, Kimberly peeked through the blind on the front picture window to make sure the coast was clear outside the house. Walking to the switch by the front door, she dimmed the ceiling light, turned the bolt, and confided, "Todd's in Washington visiting a friend, and can't possibly show up here anytime soon." Now I knew what her intentions were.

The past weeks had been hell for me, even worse than when Kimberly broke the news about Todd in the spring. I bore him no grudge. He was a decent man who had the impeccable good taste to want what I thought was my own. I'd surrendered the most precious thing in my life to him. I wasn't asking him to return her. All I wanted now was Kimberly's love and affection when the opportunity arose. After all, I thought, I had a prior claim on her heart. As long as she felt the same way about me, I had no qualms about taking my due.

Kimberly found a long-playing record of Beethoven's Ninth Symphony and put it on the stereo. My initial hesitation dispelled, I grabbed her and pressed my lips to hers, igniting the passion still burning inside us. We hugged and kissed, and slowly undressed each other. Stark naked and relishing the sensation of our bare flesh, we lay down on the carpeted floor and continued to caress. With this need fulfilled, I moved on top of her to regain the intimacy we longed for.

Never in all the times we made love did I feel a greater closeness to her than I felt that night. The setting was spartan, the soft light, erotic, and the music, hypnotic, as if Beethoven himself hovered over us, conducting. We foresaw only this one chance to be together, so we took it slow and paced ourselves to make our pleasure last. With her body at one with mine, our lovemaking ebbed and flowed with the glorious music. At the end of the magnificent crescendo, we, too, climaxed on the final note. Thus concluded the one and only musical soirée I attended at Todd Johnson's house.

On the way back to Fairlington, I told Kimberly what my schedule would be for the next two weeks. I was going to stay at my Grandma Wertime's until it was time to take Dick to Haverford for new student orientation on September twentieth, then I would return to my grandmother's house until September twenty-fifth, when I had to start my sophomore year.

Kimberly said she would write to me, but that I should immediately destroy any letters she sent. I promised to do that, and did so very diligently. However, one of her letters ended up in the wrong hands, causing hard feelings among some in the Wertime clan and significant problems for me.

As far back as I can remember, my grandmother, Flora Montgomery Wertime, took a special interest in me as the oldest of her many grandchildren, and I loved her dearly. She had long brown hair like Kimberly's, which she wore in braids wrapped around her head. Grandma's face was sweet, almost angelic. She fed me well the many times I stayed with her. My good, hardworking Presbyterian grandmother, the mainstay of the family, was there for everybody. She wanted her progeny to succeed in life and make it to heaven. One couldn't ask for a better grandmother than she.

Early in August 1960, before my parents and brothers departed for Iran, a rare event occurred in the Wertime family—we all congregated at the Mountain Place at the same time for a picnic and portrait. My reunion with Kimberly at Todd's house was no less a welcome surprise. It did nothing, however, to lessen my anguish and need to be in touch—to know that Kimberly still loved me.

As she said she would, Kimberly wrote me several times at Grandma Wertime's house that September. At the end of each letter, she indicated when she would send another, so I could be on the lookout for it. With the sound of each passing car on the appointed day, I hurried down the walk along the side of my grandmother's house to the mailbox on the street, hoping the mailman had just been there on his rural delivery.

When a letter from Kimberly arrived, I rushed upstairs to my bedroom and closed the door. As I opened her letter and read its contents, I could hardly contain my excitement. Despite what she had said about having to love me in a different way, words proved easier than action. She now had a new husband, but still needed me. Kimberly wrote openly about her feelings, about how much she cared for me and missed me, and that when it came to making love, Todd couldn't compare.

On an appointed day, to my surprise, a letter from Kimberly didn't arrive, and I knew no reason why. For a couple of days, I paced and stewed, then had to leave for Arlington to pick up Dick. The following morning, when I was back at Grandma's and nervously awaiting the letter, an aunt and uncle of mine, who lived nearby, unexpectedly entered the kitchen. They summoned me to the parlor, a room rarely used, but in which we grandchildren played with a set of building blocks all of us loved.

At the far end, I saw three chairs arranged side by side, with a single one in front. My uncle invited me to have a seat as the three of them sat facing me. After a moment of silence, he addressed me with a question.

"John, do you know why we're here today?" he asked.

"No," I replied, "I have no idea what this is all about."

"We know you've been carrying on immorally with that Kimberly," he began. "She's a married woman who'll be your ruination. We've seen what she's doing to you. Mother says you've acted strangely ever since you got here, that you seem to be pining away, almost as if you're under a spell. This has to stop before it does you further harm!"

My uncle then continued, "I've tracked her down and called her on the phone. I told her to leave our boy alone, and if she doesn't, I'll press charges against her!!" To all of this, my grandmother and aunt nodded their agreement.

Sitting there facing relatives I'd known all my life and for whom I had great affection, I could hardly believe my eyes and ears. At first, I didn't know what to say. But it was obvious what they had done—one of them purloined the letter I awaited, and in the process, committed a federal crime.

My protective reflexes now kicked into gear. I wasn't about to admit to these charges and endanger Kimberly and her girls.

"Uncle, you've got it all wrong! Kimberly and I are just good friends who confide in each other. I've known her and her daughters for years. I used to babysit for them. She's my mother's best friend, not someone I'm romantically involved with. You met her at the Mountain Place and seemed to like her a lot."

From his long experience in dealing with evidence and people who don't always tell the truth, my uncle looked me in the eye and let me know he didn't believe me.

"If I'm mistaken," he said, "you come by at any time and tell me I was wrong!"

"I will," I said.

"Okay, I'll be waiting," he replied, and with that, rested my relatives' case against Kimberly and me.

Grandma Wertime remained seated as my aunt and uncle rose and prepared to depart. Having heard these harsh charges leveled against the one I loved, I was reeling inside, and didn't know what to do. The only thing that came to mind was to stand up and kiss my grandmother on her forehead, something I'd never done before, but which made her beam with satisfaction. Perhaps she thought she was helping to save a young man from the claws of a Lilith and certain perdition. I knew she loved me and was trying to protect me, as were my uncle and aunt, but the way they chose to do it, on top of all I'd been through the previous weeks, only made me more distraught.

I couldn't pick up and leave, because there was no place to go, and no one with whom I could talk. I couldn't even use the phone to call Kimberly. My only recourse was to stay and suffer in silence.

That night, and for some nights to come, I lay in bed, tossing and turning, and wondering about Kimberly. To think that my uncle had found and threatened her that way was too much to bear. He could easily have ruined her marriage and the life she was trying to provide her girls. Their well-being was the most important thing to me. The more I thought, the angrier I got, until I took pen in hand and began to write my parents.

I pulled out all the stops. I told them of the inquisition that had taken place in Grandma Wertime's parlor, how hurt I was they'd think ill of Kimberly and me for being good, but innocent, friends. I reminded them that my aunt and uncle had both met Kim and her daughters at the Mountain Place, where my uncle took a shine to our guest, along with the other men. Furthermore, I asked, why did they have to pick on a homeless college student who thought he'd done the family proud with his good work at Haverford? This and more went off to Iran.

At the same time, I later learned from my mother, Grandma Wertime sent my father an irate letter of her own. In it, she quoted from a letter Kimberly had written to me, which proved, Grandma said, we were sleeping together and carrying on immorally. Scandalized by our behavior, Grandma wanted it stopped at once, with none of "Peg's shilly-shallying interfering."

Seeing the handiwork of one of his sisters in this, my father was furious at what he thought was a canard leveled at Kimberly and me, and wrote back angrily, telling them in no uncertain terms to leave us alone. Then he told my mother, "I wish John and Kimberly had done what they're accused of doing! *That would serve the family right!*" In a letter to me, Dad expressed his confidence in me and my story and his disgust with those meddling in my affairs and impugning Kimberly's good name.

During the few days left before I returned to Haverford, I could hardly move, so great was the devastation I felt. To help lift me out of the daze I was in, my aunt suggested I visit a local college with her to meet some of the girls in residence. She knew one who spoke French, which I had done well in my freshman year and enjoyed speaking very much. Nevertheless, after the trauma of the preceding weeks, I found I could no longer carry on a conversation in that language, which demoralized me even more. To make matters worse, I was scheduled to live in Haverford's French House and was registered to take a French literature course that would start in a week.

I desperately wanted to call Kimberly, but hesitated for fear someone might be listening in. I didn't feel safe in writing her, either, so great was my paranoia. Until I left for school, I felt isolated and trapped.

On Sunday, the twenty-fifth, I settled into French House, one of the big old residences across from the Duck Pond, not far from the main entrance to the campus. My French professor the previous year, Brad Cook, and his family, lived on the first floor in an apartment behind a sitting room and staircase we students used. Several small rooms, including mine, were upstairs above the Cooks, and above us were still others. From the front door of French House to Founders Hall was a good ten-minute walk, which I enjoyed for the beauty of the campus lawns and trees, and the exercise it gave me.

Relieved to be where our personal business was secure, I telephoned Kimberly from the public phone in the hall next to my room. I made my call during the day when I though she'd be alone. The timing was right. On my first try, I got her. The sound of her voice raised my spirits.

"How *are* you, Kimberly?" I asked anxiously.

"Johnny!" she cried with joy, "I'm okay, how are *you* doing?"

"I survived an inquisition," I answered, "and learned about my uncle's terrible threat to you."

168

"It was awful, Johnny," Kimberly exclaimed. "He said he'd tell Todd about us and take legal action against me. I was petrified thinking of the damage it would do to everyone. I told him you and Peggy are my dearest friends, and that I'd never do anything to harm either one of you. Thank God he didn't carry through!"

Hearing her voice again, the angst that had built up inside me found some release. In subsequent correspondence and calls, I was able to catch up on the news of her life, how the girls were doing, and what Todd's department and teaching were like.

At the first meeting of my modern French literature course with Jacques Mariès, a visiting professor from France, and five other students, my newfound inability to express myself orally was readily apparent. After a couple of classes, I talked with M. Mariès about my loss of self-confidence and concluded I should drop his course. A quiet, somewhat shy, person, he urged me to stay with it anyhow since I understood what was said in class and could write French well enough. I took his advice, learned a lot, and got a good grade, but after that, dropped my study of French. A year later, Brad Cook asked my brother, Dick, why I wasn't taking any more French courses. At the time I couldn't tell my brother the reason.

In November, I learned from Kimberly that Grandma Schultz was back in Fairlington. The truth of what my grandmother often repeated, "Remember, the grass looks greener on the other side," came home to her at considerable heartache and expense. Her old friends in California, on whom she'd counted, didn't welcome her the way they did when she and my grandfather lived nearby. Realizing her mistake, Grandma telephoned Kimberly in tears and asked for her help. My grandmother's return was a godsend to me, since my only alternative for a place to stay was Grandma Wertime's house. In her new home, Grandma Schultz no longer had her dog. With no place to keep him in California, she sent him to Tehran. My maternal grandmother was very good to me the many times she lodged and fed me. I believe she enjoyed my company, too.

At the Thanksgiving, Christmas, and spring vacations that year, Dick and I filled our old station wagon with paying customers to the

Washington area. Due to all the hauling it had done, its shock absorbers and steering linkage were pretty well shot. On certain stretches of road, the car swayed from side to side, hammock-like, as I drove along. The first time it happened, one of our passengers looked terrified. I'm not sure he ever relaxed while riding with us, but it was convenient and inexpensive, so he never gave it up.

As survivors of the inquisition, Kimberly and I had another bond. Although we wrote and often called, that wasn't enough. We had to see one another again. To my delight, she invited me to come for a visit during spring break. On March twenty-fifth, our classes recessed for a week, Dick and I headed to Fairlington. The next day, my brother drove me to Union Station in Alexandria, where I boarded a southbound train.

When I alighted before dawn, Kimberly and Todd met me along the track. I apologized for inconveniencing them so early in the morning, but Kimberly said they'd gotten used to it, because "a lot of university visitors come down to our little southern town this way." They took me home, where I went to bed in a guest room off the kitchen.

After napping a couple of hours, I got up and came out to find Kimberly preparing breakfast the way she did in Fairlington. With a sparkling smile, she gave me a hug and a hearty welcome. I couldn't take my eyes off her—she was as dazzling as ever. We chattered away about our families and what living in the South was like. When the phone rang, she got tied up in conversation, which gave me an opportunity to look around the house and poke my head outside.

It was much warmer there than it was in Philadelphia and Washington. All the trees were green. I came across Todd reading *Pravda* in the living room, where I could see Kimberly's decorative flair at work. Some of the furniture I recognized from before. Other pieces were obviously Todd's. Something I coveted stood in front of the sofa he sat on. It was an enormous coffee table, made, Todd told me, for one of the old robber barons. There were other interesting things I hadn't seen, such as an elaborately carved medieval high back chair and a large wooden chest of similar ilk. On the wall were paintings and art objects he'd bought at auction in Washington. Kimberly had found herself a cultured man with excellent taste. Todd was cordial enough to his young visitor, asking me about my parents, and how they liked Tehran.

Jill and Martie eventually woke up and came into the breakfast room of their spacious new home. We were glad to see each other again, but didn't hug or kiss. I could see the girls had grown since late August. I even heard in their voices signs of a southern drawl. I wanted to know about their school, new friends, and what they did with themselves. They had obviously adapted well to their new surroundings and life with Todd, who called them "the chicks." I, too, was forced to adapt, although I didn't like it. This was not like old times, when I had Kimberly all to myself, but it was better than nothing.

With her good looks and the warmth she exuded, Kimberly was well suited to southern living. One of the first things she told me was, "Johnny, you don't know how different things are down here in the South. The way southern men relate to women, the way women talk to each other, and how they think. It's all quite a revelation. Before you leave, you'll see what I'm talking about. We're going to have a party here next week after a lecture by James Schlesinger from the University of Virginia." I looked forward to that and to looking around as much as I could. More than anything, however, I was hoping to see some hospitality from Kimberly herself, which I'd longed for since our musical soirée.

In the early afternoon, the girls left the house on an errand. Then Todd departed unexpectedly to do some work in his office. Seeing this, we realized we had an opportunity that wouldn't last long. Ducking into her room, Kimberly soon reappeared wearing a skirt. With barely enough time for a quickie, we embraced in my bedroom standing up. A second after we climaxed, someone called out "Mom." As Kimberly instinctively pulled back, the seed I'd planted in her plopped out onto my pants. She quickly composed herself and went out to greet her girls. I scrounged around for some Kleenex, then got into another pair of trousers. We had reestablished intimacy, but needed a safer place for making love.

Tuesday evening, Kimberly and I went with Todd to the university to hear Professor Schlesinger speak on a highly technical aspect of nuclear defense. After it was over, many of those present went back to Todd's and Kimberly's house, where I met some of their colleagues and friends. While eating chips and conversing on the enclosed porch, I started an argument over the utility of education in promoting development in third world countries. The debate went on for some time as Dr. Schlesinger stood by and watched. His topic that evening had elicited little follow-up discussion. It was the issue I raised that worked everyone up. I also conversed with one of their non-academic guests, an older gentleman and native southerner, from whom I got a sense of the local aristocracy. When everyone had gone and Kimberly was cleaning up, she remarked, "You sure conducted yourself admirably in the discussion tonight, Johnny!" I was proud she thought so, and had enjoyed myself.

While Todd was teaching and the girls were in school, Kimberly gave me a tour of their town. We visited the university campus as well as a small art museum to which Todd had donated some objects. Another day, Kimberly and I headed out into the countryside, where there was a riding stable and ring. While I had the first horseback ride of my life, she galloped along side me and all over the place. When we got home, my legs and backside were sore. I didn't hanker for more riding, but was happy to have done it once.

On the last day of my stay, we drove a short distance out of town to an area where men went to hunt in the fall. During that season, Kimberly told me, one had to be careful of quicksand, in which hunters were known to have perished. As we walked over the sandy soil dotted with scrub pines, I felt apprehensive, but Kimberly calmed my fears. The sun had risen high in the sky and the day was warm and welcoming. We found a soft, grassy spot where we could lie down out of sight to relax, and to make love. As we had experienced before, there's no better way than *en plein air*.

Watching Kimberly prepare dinner and move about the house that night, I knew I wanted her companionship and love more than anything in the world. She loved and needed me, too, I thought, but I could see her marriage and interesting life had changed our situation drastically. Although I didn't want to admit it, my hold on her was fast slipping away.

I returned to Alexandria on the train. The day after I arrived, my brother and I thanked our grandmother and drove back to Haverford to finish out the year. As had happened the previous spring vacation,

I missed being with Kim on my birthday by just a week. This April ninth was a particular milestone—I was no longer a teenager. Soon, she would be thirty-eight.

In early June, not long before Dick, Grandma Schultz, and I were to leave on a summer-long trip to Iran, Kimberly called me one evening at my grandmother's house to say she and Todd were at a hotel in Washington. Todd had some consulting to do and she had come up with him. Kimberly wondered if I was free to drop by for a brief hello. I was, for her, at any time of the day or night, so we made plans to meet at their room in the late morning.

Smartly dressed in a coat and tie for our rendezvous, I knocked on their door. Todd had gone off to a meeting, but was expecting Kimberly to join him for lunch, which left us only a short time together. I was dying to hold Kim again. As soon as I did, I wanted to go all the way. While hesitating to get undressed for fear her husband might return, Kimberly also wanted to satisfy me, so she pushed me back onto a chair, unzipped my fly, and performed fellatio on me. The intensity of the sensation nearly blew my mind. For a few minutes to come, I could hardly walk, and when I did, I felt as if I was floating on air.

Kimberly had never done that before. Perhaps she feared I would like it too much. More likely, she didn't want us to be apart when we made love and miss out on her own pleasure. Our times together over the years had been relatively few and limited in duration. This added to the thrill of our dalliances, but made them all the more precious. Being satisfied individually could never take the place of ecstacy together. So true was this that the one time I happened to rub her to climax truly upset her, and she chastised me for doing it, saying, "Johnny, I wanted to go over a mountain *with you!*"

Aware that Todd could suddenly appear, we didn't hug or kiss on the street, but squeezed each other's hands as we prepared to part. Kimberly knew Dick, Grandma, and I would be leaving soon for Tehran. She wished us a bon voyage, told me to give her dear friend, Peggy, a hug and kiss for her, and pass on her love to Dad, Steve, and Charlie. Then I watched her walk away. It would be another three months before we met again, but under less happy circumstances for me.

## 26  Final Visits

As dependents of a diplomat at a foreign post, Dick and I were entitled to a trip at government expense to see our family once during our college careers. This would be our first time abroad, indeed, my first time to fly. The only thing that didn't appeal to me about the trip was being far away from Kimberly. Through USIA, we obtained diplomatic passports and first-class tickets. Grandma Schultz didn't get these perks, so she had to travel on a regular passport and pay her own way. In the plane going to Rome, Grandma felt demeaned, and cried at having "to sit in back with the plebeians" while Dick and I, like young diplomats, had seats up front and enjoyed first-class service.

During our two days in Rome, Dick, Grandma, and I saw what we could of the great sights. From there, we flew to Istanbul. This Ottoman city, old Constantinople, was as fascinating to me as Rome, but more exotic and to my taste. While exploring the great Covered Bazaar with a guide and other tourists, I fancied an old Greek Orthodox icon in one of its many small shops. In my first negotiation in a *suq*, I haggled so long, our tour guide had to come back from the bus to fetch me. To top it off, I didn't have enough money in my pocket to pay for the piece, so the gracious young guide, a handsome Turk named Yilmaz, told the dealer he would collect from me at the hotel and pay him later.

Our flight from Istanbul put us into Tehran late at night. Crossing over eastern Turkey and western Iran, we saw few signs of life until we got to the capital city, whose clear, bright lights sparkling in the dry desert air made for an unforgettable sight. Mother, Dad, Steve, and Charlie were at Mehrabad Airport to greet us. In our many conversations about what we'd all done during the previous nine months, no one said a word about the inquisition.

Dad was an inveterate traveler. He toured many parts of Iran on USIA business, for scholarly research, or personal pleasure, often with Mother and Charlie along. On one of the trips we took as a family, we descended a winding dirt road with hairpin turns from the high, arid Iranian plateau to the lush, green sub-tropical Caspian Sea region with its rice paddies and thatched roof houses.

Another time, Dad, my brothers, and I headed south to Esfahan over a washboard-like dirt road, which passing vehicles turned into sufficating clouds of dust. Esfahan's monumental central square, once a polo field, with the covered bazaar, Safavid-era palace and domed mosques surrounding it, made a lasting impression on me.

Along the road to Shiraz, Iran's most pleasant southern city, we stopped at the ruins of Pasargadae, site of the capital and tomb of Cyrus the Great. Beyond that was the Marvdasht plain, where Persepolis, the Achaemenian kings' ritual capital, lay in ruins since Alexander the Great burned it in 330 BC. A custom I found so strange in Iranian cities—of young men locking pinkies while walking together—became clearer when I saw the same carved in bas-relief on Persepolis' monumental staircase.

That summer, Dick and I taught English at the Iran-America Society. To commute to work, we took a taxi to the center of the city and back. Each time we did, we had to haggle over the fare since cabs had no meters. The Persian we learned and spoke came mainly from pointers Dad gave us and from negotiating with our drivers.

The many exciting new places and things I saw and experienced that summer didn't divert my mind from the woman I loved. I thought of Kimberly constantly when I was alone or in bed, and communicated with her by mail through the APO. I had seen what her life with Todd was like and how she thrived as a professor's wife. She had opportunities and things I could never give her and her girls. I was happy for them, but felt threatened by what I found, and was desperate to maintain the small hold I still had on her.

Now, for the first time since her marriage, I began to feel possessive. In letters I sent, I made claims on Kimberly that she found upsetting, like wanting to have exclusive control of her love, and being the

175

only one to give her true sexual pleasure. My intention was to end my trip abroad by going to see her and taking up where we had left off in the spring.

Kim responded that I was welcome to come, but indicated her unhappiness at the tone of my letters. "Johnny," she wrote, "you've got to understand I'm married to Todd and am in his debt for all he's given me and my girls. We have a growing relationship that's also affectionate. It's not fair to expect me not to respond to his kindness." That was a message I didn't want to hear. I was determined to assert what I considered to be my prior claim, irrespective of all that had transpired during the previous year.

In late August, Grandma Schultz and Steve left together for Arlington. Dick took off on his own, and I, soon after. On my homeward journey, I made seven stops in sixteen days, all before New York, Washington, and Kimberly's abode. By the time I reached her home, I hardly knew what I was doing. My first night there, I woke up shouting in the dark. Hearing me cry out, Kimberly and Todd rushed in to see what was going on. When they turned on the light, they found me completely disoriented. To Kimberly's question, "Johnny, what's wrong?" all I could do was to ask, "Where am I?" Hearing her voice and seeing them there, I knew I'd finally reached my goal, and promptly fell asleep again.

In the strong summer light the next morning, I regained my bearings, especially once I laid eyes on the woman I loved. Full of smiles, Kimberly kidded me about my nightmarish cries, asking in jest if her "little old town" hadn't caused them. I told her and Todd about my summer in Iran, places I'd visited and people I'd met. I had a present for them that was was too big to carry with me. When it arrived from Iran, I mailed it to them.

Kimberly was her bright and bubbly self, but her feelings toward me weren't what they had been in the spring. No doubt, the expectations I voiced in my correspondence from Iran bothered her. When I held her and kissed her I didn't see the old eagerness to reciprocate or go further. One time, we went out of town to a place that reminded me of an old quarry. I was dying to make love to her there, but the spot wasn't isolated enough and she demurred. To free herself of the pressure I exerted, she satisfied me manually. I was relieved of the tension that had built up inside me, but knew she hadn't done this out of pleasure or love. Whether I liked it or not, our relationship had changed. After a few disappointing days, I was ready to return to Virginia. Kimberly took me to the airport for my flight home. I had to get ready for college.

During the the second semester of my junior year, my father made a suggestion that intrigued me—I take a year off to go live in Tehran with them, study Persian, teach English, and travel. My experience the previous summer whetted my appetite for this, so I obtained a leave of absence from the college.

Kim and I continued to correspond from time to time. I missed her desperately, and hoped our relationship wasn't completely dead. Before I returned to Iran, I had to see her again. I heard about some students who were looking for riders to Florida at the beginning of the spring break. I called to see if Kimberly would welcome a visit, and got a warm response. The Haverford students I rode with dropped me off on the way, and she picked me up. I brought along the old Greek icon I bought in the Istanbul bazaar. It had hung on my wall in French House since September. I wanted Kimberly to have it as a secret token of my love for her and a special reminder of me.

My stay was cordial enough, the way it is with old friends, but had none of the intimacy I craved. During my visit, I met a couple who were close to Kimberly and Todd, with whom they played a truncated version of tennis on a three-quarter sized court in the back yard. I joined them in playing doubles, but couldn't help hitting the ball too far. The husband was a sharp and personable man, a physician no less.

The fourteen months I spent in Iran were formative ones for my future interests and life. When I returned for my final year of college, I was set on a new course of study. As a Haverford student, I was able to take Persian and Arabic at the University of Pennsylvania. Later that year, I won two fellowships to study at Princeton's graduate school.

In the spring of 1964, two years after I had last seen her, I went again to visit the woman who enthralled me. Kimberly was her usual gracious self and seemed pleased to have me back. As before, we played that maddening version of tennis with the doctor and his wife, and had pleasant chats. I longed for Kimberly's love, as I always did, but her fling with youth was over now, and she had weaned herself from me.

Taking after their mother, Jill and Martie were pretty girls. One day when Kimberly was out of the house, fifteen-and-a-half-year-old Martie fixed me some lunch—a big plate of pasta and rice. In chatting with Martie about herself and her friends, I made a stupid crack with sexual innuendos—exactly what I don't recall. I had a female on my mind, not either of those who grew up with me like little sisters, but someone unknown, someone I needed to find. Martie had never heard me speak this way before—I never had to when her mother and I were lovers—and became upset, as I soon found out. She probably didn't know it, but where there's talk, there's little action, which was now my problem. After this awkward incident, Kimberly came to me with a look of concern, and said, "Johnny, Martie's asked me, 'Is something wrong with Johnny, is he sick?'"

Yes, Kimberly, I was sick, indeed, suffering from loneliness and longing that bordered on starvation. If Kimberly had forgotten what it was like to be that way, how could I ever explain it? All I needed from her to help soothe my pain was a few words of recognition—that what we had been and done together was as meaningful to her as it was to me, more than fleeting pleasure, something she would remember and treasure forever. But life had changed for her, and she was no longer the same.

I stayed another day, then knew it was time to leave. With a perfunctory embrace from Kimberly, I boarded the train for Virginia. Sitting there watching her wave, I came to a final acceptance—the bliss I'd known during my coming of age was over; my hope for a life with Kimberly abandoned. The whistle blew and the train pulled away. I felt alone and lonely again, back where I was when I was fifteen—longing for someone to hold and to love, to call my very own. In self-defense, my only recourse was to try to forget her.

# Improbable Love

## Epilogue

As I watched my mother from across the dinner table one evening late in the spring of 2006, I saw dullness in her face instead of the old sparkle and smile I was used to. My father's untimely death from cancer in 1982 had nothing to do with her decline; rather, it started with a fall and broken hip many years later. When she regained mobility, Mother was no longer comfortable driving or handling her daily affairs, which fell to me. Together with my brother, Charles, who lived in her home, Mother walked down the street to our house for dinner every day, and back again, weather permitting. Deeper into her eighties, even this short stroll became too difficult for her to manage.

While driving her home that evening, I instinctively felt my mother was entering the final phase of her life, and that the time had come for me to unburden myself of my long-held secret. Before I helped her into the house, I reminded Mother that she once asked Kimberly if she and I were sleeping together, but never got a straightforward answer. I then revealed the truth about us, to which she showed no surprise or emotion. Just inside the front door, however, she turned to me in wide-eyed animation, and said, "*Tell me more!*" I explained that I was writing a memoir about our relationship, and that she could best learn the details by reading the manuscript when completed. She never said another word to me about this, but did mention it to Charles. Her death in early December precluded the opportunity.

That autumn, while my mother was in a nursing home, I got an unexpected call from Kimberly's daughter, Martie, informing me that Kimberly had died of cancer in July, and that she and Jill were planning an early December memorial for their mother. At the time of her death, Kimberly was married to the doctor I had met when he and his former wife played doubles with Kimberly and Todd. Kimberly's marriage to

180

Todd ended in divorce in the early 1970s. Todd died in 1979. Kimberly's marriage to the doctor was a happy, loving one. "As a mature woman," her older daughter wrote, "she was the pillar of the community, the person everyone came to for advice, comfort, laughter and friendship."

I had a strong urge to attend Kimberly's memorial, but knew I couldn't because of my mother's precarious condition. I also didn't want to be in a position of having to conceal the true nature of our relationship. The only immediate members of our families who knew our secret before Mother did were my wife, Suzan, and my brother, Dick, who in surprise nearly hit the roof of the car I was driving when I told him about us.

Following my two sojourns in Iran in the early 1960s, I returned to Tehran in 1968 as a Princeton University graduate student to research a doctoral dissertation on Iranian history. During my eight-year residence, I taught English to support myself, traveled extensively in Iran, Afghanistan, Turkey and Greece, and became a serious collector and student of nomadic textile art, about which I began to write and curate exhibitions. Although I did a considerable amount of work on my dissertation, I gradually became more and more involved with my love for textiles, which determined my lifelong career as a writer, dealer, curator, lecturer, appraiser, and consultant in the antique rug and textile art field.

While residing in Tehran, I met a beautiful, charming, and intelligent Persian twelve years my junior, whom I married in 1973. Before our marriage, I informed Suzan of my earlier relationship with Kimberly, which she accepted with grace and understanding. Our first son, Sam, was born in Tehran in 1976, shortly before we moved to Virginia. Eight years after him, our second son, Daryush, was born, and four years later, our daughter, Shirin. All are well-adjusted and well-educated individuals leading interesting and productive lives. From Sam and our daughter-in-law, Kate, Suzan and I now also have the joy of a young granddaughter, Audrey. What Kimberly told me on several occasions when I despaired of losing her—that one day I would have a beautiful young wife and family—happily came true.

Twenty years elapsed between my visit to Kimberly in 1964 and our next meeting. This came about when Suzan, Sam, and I, along with my brother Steve's young son spent a pleasant night and morning with her and her doctor husband in their home on our way to the Atlantic shore. By then, Kimberly had had a double mastectomy and a metal plate put in her skull, where an intruder in their home had viciously hit her. Despite this, she still looked very fit and attractive, and maintained her cheerful outlook on life.

After that, I saw Kimberly only twice, once when she and Jill stopped by our house in Fairlington for a short visit, and another time when she and the doctor came by to say hello. There was also the occasional letter or greeting card, phone call at Christmas time, brief chat when I happened to be at my mother's while the two of them were conversing on the phone, or sporadic calls from her to me or me to her.

Over the years after we parted, the thrill and hurt I felt with Kimberly remained alive deep inside me, and surfaced after I heard her voice or something jogged my memory. To try to understand Kimberly's continuing hold on me, not long before my sixtieth birthday, with Suzan's knowledge and support, I put my work aside and regressed to the distant past. For several months, as if in a trance, I relived in my mind my experiences as a child and as a youth with my lover. While doing this, I fell in love again with the Kimberly I had known and longed for her once more, so powerful was my regression. These unexpected emotions surprised Suzan and me and made us wonder where my quest for insight was leading me.

Those who read what I had just recorded during this episode had different thoughts about the meaning of my experience, and what I should do about revealing it. As time went by, I grappled with these reactions and with the lack of opportunity to engage in unguarded conversation with Kimberly. I longed to reestablish the verbal intimacy we once enjoyed, but also felt a reticence, and certain vulnerability, in exposing the feelings of love and hurt I still harbored for her, and the questions some readers were raising about our relationship. In retrospect, I believe the need I had on my final visit to Kimberly in the early 1960s was never resolved. This missed connection and the urge to express what I was unable to tell her directly, and wanted to hear from her in turn, underlie this remembrance of our improbable love. With her death went the possibility of fulfilling my need. The only solace I'm left with is what Martie told me the day she called to inform me of Kimberly's passing, "Mom talked about you all the time."

Some who have read or heard my story have suggested that what I experienced with Kimberly was a clear case of exploitation or child abuse. In my youth and for a long time afterward, I never thought of this as a possibility, despite the warning I had from Coach. After much inner struggle, I still believe Kimberly was as much in love with me as I was with her, and in no way did she intend to take advantage of me, or act out of selfishness or malice.

A skeptic might respond that intent is not the issue here; rather, it is the reality of what she did, and the fact that after so many years have passed, I have felt the need to address our relationship as I have in this book. This may be a valid point, but if the life I've lived since the end of our relationship exhibits no lasting damage, can one speak of abuse? Perhaps this is the rationalization of an abused person covering for his abuser. In my heart and mind, however, I don't believe this to be the case.

Several people have asked me the question, "Would you want a son of yours to experience what you did with Kimberly?" As a responsible adult and parent, I would have to answer no. I wouldn't want him to suffer the pain I did in trying to leap ahead of my years. I wouldn't want to see my son experience the anguish and desolation I felt at times, or face moral dilemmas of the kind that confronted me before I was ready to act responsibly. Rather, I would want him to grow up and discover love at his own pace, and to develop socially and intellectually with as few burdens as possible. In short, I would want him to be an adolescent until ready for adulthood.

If, however, one asks whether I would willingly undo the relationship I had with Kimberly if it were possible, I'd answer emphatically, "I would not." A more conventional life than what I led in my youth wouldn't have fit the person I was. I believe I was lucky both to have had a loving relationship of the kind I did and to have escaped significant harm from it. Many others in my position might not have fared as well. The potential for lasting damage is real when a naïve youth encounters an experienced adult in such an intimate and enduring way.

Falling in love as a highly impressionable and callow fifteen-year-old boy and living intimately and secretively for a considerable length of time with a woman eighteen years older was a transforming experience. It was very different from the one I have had from the age of thirty-one married to a woman much younger than me. Few people can claim to have had both kinds of relationships. The first helped me better understand the second; both have made me a better partner and person. I feel privileged to have lived with, and loved, both women.

## Acknowledgments

The understanding and unstinting support of my wife, Suzan, and the unflagging editing and encouragement of our friend, Jane Merrill, made this book possible. I dedicate it to them, *the ones who believed.*

The comments and reaction, whether positive or negative, encouraging or discouraging, of each person who read a version of my story, or heard only the gist of it, over the past ten years, gave me food for thought and helped impel me to persevere. Early readers were Elizabeth Callard, Richard Arndt, Maggie Lee, Amanda Urban, and Richard A. Wertime. The last of these, my brother, Dick, author of *Citadel on the Mountain* and professor of English literature at Arcadia University, called my attention to American society's evolved understanding of, and less willingness to tolerate, child sexual abuse compared to our youth. He also posed questions that challenged me to think about my experience in ways I had not.

Later readers were Diane Freed, Teri Tobias, Fred Mushkat, Julia Hough, Andrew Maltz, Leah Fry, Virginia Seacrist, Barbara Selfridge, Vivian, and Pat. From some I gained insights into how to present the story, from others, encouragement that I had connected with him or her in some significant way, or both.

In employing his skills gained as a professional psychologist, my friend, Andrew D. Maltz, Ph.D., played a significant role in helping me think through the meaning of child abuse in relation to my particular experience, and also in helping me come to a resolution of conflicted feelings. He further proved to be a patient and highly sensitive editor of the opening and closing parts of my book.

Virginia Seacrist, Ginny Jacobs in our high school days, used her long experience as a writer and skills as an editor and teacher of

English to raise important questions and to suggest a new approach to opening my story. In crucial places she helped with wording and challenged me to think further.

Marcia Satterthwaite, friend, relative, and mental health professional, offered helpful advice and insights based on conversations we had.

With his technical expertise, Arthur Feller prepared the cover, images, and text for the printer. He also provided sound editorial advice.

To all of the above, my sincere thanks for the time and effort they spent with me, with my manuscript, or both. What appears in print here, in the final analysis, is what I think and feel, and for which I accept full responsibility.

**Photographic credits.**

Cover photograph: At the Mountain Place, August 1959 (Polaroid).

Page 2. Wertime family.

Page 5. John Wertime.

Page 11. John Wertime.

Page 64. Wertime family.

Page 88. From the 1958 Wakefield High School *Starstone*, used with permission.

Page 142. Wertime family.

CPSIA information can be obtained at www.ICGtesting.com
230954LV00007B/1/P